"The Bible is the living and active Word of God—
Chris and Katie take the reader by the hand and c
With the FOCUSed15 approach, in just fifteen minu
that the Lord is good."

—**HEATHER MACFADYEN,** host of the God Centered Mom podcast

"Men and women are searching for discipleship tools for themselves or others they are dis-
cipling. Chris and Katie Orr have delivered up a fresh, substantive tool to accomplish both.
FOCUSed15 is a serious study method that is possible even for those with demanding
responsibilities. This material will fit in a variety of settings for men and women everywhere
on their spiritual journey."

—**DR. ED LITTON,** pastor of Redemption Church, Mobile, AL,
and **KATHY LITTON,** NAMB consultant leading ministry to pastors' wives

"Jonah is a book, rich with lessons, that guides us as we walk with Jesus in and through real
life. Thankfully, Chris and Katie Orr have done the hard work of helping us understand and
apply those lessons to our lives in immediate and impactful ways. You should get this study
and drink deeply from the Word of God as it is found in the Book of Jonah."

—**MICAH FRIES,** senior pastor, Brainerd Baptist Church, Chattanooga, TN

"Chris and Katie Orr have the gift of writing relatable, rich Bible studies that not only
reveals Scripture in new ways but also teach me how to keep studying it on my own. The
FOCUSed15 studies are simple enough for me to complete even when my schedule is
crazy, and yet they are deep enough to allow me to linger in the Word as well."

—**KAT LEE,** author of *Hello Mornings* and founder of HelloMornings.org

"The FOCUSed15 studies do something most others don't: they force you into the Bible,
and that makes them absolutely priceless. Pick up a copy for yourself—or better yet, grab
a handful, and dive into the Word with your friends. You'll be glad you did."

—**ELYSE FITZPATRICK,** author and conference speaker

"Chris and Katie Orr have designed devotional material that leads the reader to encounter
the biblical text with guidance that reinforces solid principles of biblical interpretation and
helpful application that makes God's Word come alive in our daily choices."

—**TREVIN WAX,** Bible and Reference Publisher for LifeWay,
author, and general editor of *The Gospel Project*

OTHER BOOKS IN THE
FOCUSed15 Bible study series

PHILIPPIANS
Engage God's Purposes.
Encounter His Peace.
Experience Renewed Joy.

EVERYDAY *obedience*
Walking Purposefully in His Grace

EVERYDAY *peace*
Standing Firm in His Provision

EVERYDAY *faith*
Drawing Near to His Presence

EVERYDAY *hope*
Holding Fast to His Promise

EVERYDAY *love*
Bearing Witness to His Purpose

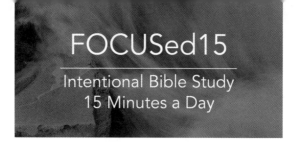

FOCUSed15

Intentional Bible Study
15 Minutes a Day

JONAH

Experience God's Patience.

Embrace His Presence.

Enjoy Divine Provision.

CHRIS and KATIE ORR

NEW HOPE®
PUBLISHERS

BIRMINGHAM, ALABAMA

New Hope® Publishers
5184 Caldwell Mill Rd.
St. 204-221
Hoover, AL 35244
NewHopePublishers.com
New Hope Publishers is a division of Iron Stream Media.

Library of Congress Cataloging-in-Publication Data

Names: Orr, Chris (Pastor), author.
Title: Jonah : experience God's patience, embrace His presence, enjoy divine
 provision / Chris and Katie Orr.
Description: First [edition]. | Birmingham : New Hope Publishers, 2018.
Identifiers: LCCN 2017058168 | ISBN 9781625915412 (permabind)
Subjects: LCSH: Bible. Jonah--Textbooks.
Classification: LCC BS1605.55 .O77 2018 | DDC 224/.920071--dc23
LC record available at https://lccn.loc.gov/2017058168

ISBN-13: 978-1-62591-541-2

18 19 20 21 22 -- 5 4 3 2 1

CONTENTS

APPENDIX

INTRODUCTION

IF YOU WERE to ask me (Chris) how I knew Katie, I could truthfully assert, "She lives on the same street as me." This statement, although true, stops well short of the fullness of our connection—it leaves out all the best stuff! We not only live on the same street, but in the same house. We not only live in the same house, but we are married, and she is the mother of my children. We are more than just street-mates. Our lives are forever entwined in ways well beyond any other person in our neighborhood. In the same way, many might say they know about the Book of Jonah, but if they stop at a simple description of the story, they will miss all the good stuff.

Most people see this small story of Jonah as one with a moral: don't run from God, or He'll send a fish to swallow you. We believe this summary falls well short of God's intended purpose for the book. The Book of Jonah has much more to hold for our everyday lives than meets the eye.

Jonah was a runner, this we all know. God said go. Jonah said no. Then he attempted to run away from the God of the universe. Yet the story continues, as Jonah seemingly learns his lesson, and God recommissions Jonah to the task at hand. Yet Jonah once again proves he had a small view of God and a stubborn heart.

Jonah chose safety over submission.

Jonah chose pride over pity.

Jonah chose comfort over compassion.

There will be much for us to prayerfully consider about our own lives. Do we look like Jonah? Are our actions and attitudes more similar to his than we care to admit?

Yet, there is also much we can learn about the character of God and our interactions with Him. In this tiny Old Testament book we see the sovereignty of God, the power of prayer, the depths of God's mercy, the richness of God's unmerited love, the lunacy of trying to escape God, the bitterness of racism, the coldness of a prophet who cares nothing for the lost, and a foreshadowing of the Savior who is to come.

We're praying your time in Jonah will be not only insightful but transformational. Along the way, we hope you'll also pick up a few tools and gain a bit of confidence to open God's Word on your own. Are you ready? Let's go.

THE NEED FOR FOCUS

IF THIS IS your first FOCUSed15 study, you'll want to carefully read through the following introduction and study method instructions. After that, we'll see you on Day 1!

It's hard to focus.

In a world filled with continual demands for my attention, I (Katie) struggle to keep a train of thought. Tasks I need to do. Appointments I need to remember. Projects I need to complete.

Yeah, it's hard to focus.

Without a good focus for my days, I wander. I lack the ability to choose well and to avoid the tyranny of the urgent. Without focus, days become a blur—tossed back and forth between the pressing and the enticing.

Why Focus Matters

I felt pretty lost during my first attempts at spending time with God in the Bible. After a few weeks of wandering around the Psalms and flipping through the New Testament, I realized I had no clue what I was doing.

It felt like a pretty big waste of time.

I knew the Bible was full of life-changing truths and life-giving promises, but I needed to learn how to focus on the details to see all that Scripture held for me.

In the medical world, we depend on the microscope. Even with all the fancy machines that can give test results in seconds, the microscope has yet to become obsolete. Some things can only be discovered through the lens of the scope. What looks like nothing to the naked eye is actually teeming with life-threatening bacteria. Even under the microscope they may not be seen at first glance. But with the smallest adjustment of the focus, the blurry cloud of the field in view is brought into focus, and the finest details are revealed.

And those details matter.

You need a microscope to make a diagnosis, but the microscope itself doesn't make the discoveries. It takes a trained eye to distinguish between cells. The average person may be able to figure out how to use the microscope to find a cell and get it in focus, but without training, the beginner will not know the clinical significance of what is seen.

Similarly, when we approach God's Word, we must learn to focus on what we see and develop a trained eye to know its significance.

Ready for More

I grew up in a shallow Christian culture. Don't do drugs. Don't have sex. Don't tell lies. Read your Bible. Be a light—sold-out for Jesus. This was the sum of being a good Christian—or so I thought. Now, I'm your typical firstborn list-checker, so the do's and don'ts worked for me . . . for a while. But as I got older and the temptations of the don'ts became more enticing, I began to wonder if this Christianity thing was worth it. Is this really what people spend their lives chasing? Seems tiring—and ultimately worthless.

Yet, God was drawing my heart—I could undeniably feel it—but I knew I was missing something. I thought I'd check out this reading-the-Bible thing. Sure, I had read a devotional or two and knew all the Bible stories, but I didn't feel I knew God Himself.

A bit nervous, I drove to the local bookstore to buy my first really nice Bible. I excitedly drove back home, headed straight to my room, opened up my leather-bound beauty, and began to read.

. . . and nothing happened.

I'm not quite certain what I was expecting, but it sure wasn't confusion and frustration. I decided to give it another try the next day and still heard nothing. I had no clue what I was reading.

In all my years of storing up the do's and don'ts in my how-to-be-a-good-Christian box, I never caught a how or why.

For years I stumbled through my black leather Bible with very little learned on the other side of it all. Yet, God was faithful to lead and speak, and I fully believe He can and does speak to us through His Word, even if we are as clueless as I was.

However, I also believe God's Word is meant to be a great catalyst in our growth, and as we pursue how to better know God through His Word, we will experience Him in deeper ways.

You and I need a healthy, rich diet of God's Word in order to grow. And as we read, study, and learn to digest the Bible, we move toward becoming more like Christ. When we pursue the nearness of God, the don'ts become lackluster compared to the life-giving promises of His Word.

A FOCUSed 15 Minutes

Over time, I learned how to use incredible Bible study tools that took my time with God in His Word to a deeper level. Yet with each method, Bible study seemed to take more and more time. Certain seasons of life allow for a leisurely time in the Bible; my experience has proven most of my days don't.

As much as I would love to find a comfy chair in my favorite local coffee shop and study God's Word for hours, it is just not often possible. I'm lucky if I can get a decent breakfast in every morning before my day starts rolling. Distractions and demands abound, and many days I have not even tried to study my Bible because I just didn't have what it would take, time-wise, to get much out of it.

Until I learned to focus.

I've learned that even the busiest of Christians can learn to focus and train their eyes to discover the life-changing truths held in Scripture. No incredibly long "quiet times" or seminary degree required.

All it takes is a focused fifteen minutes.

The method I will walk you through consists of fifteen minutes, five days a week. We will focus on the same set of verses over the course of a week, and each day of that week we will look at the passage with a different lens to gather new insights along the way.

Two Ultimate Goals

Our prayer for you as we dive into the Bible is twofold. First, we want to work ourselves out of a job. We want you to walk away from this study a bit more confident in your ability to focus on the transformational truths of Scripture on your own.

Second, we hope you will encounter our God in a deep and meaningful way through these focused fifteen minutes. The most important thing about us is what we believe about God, and our prayer is that you will more accurately understand the truths about who He is through your own study of Scripture. As you get to know our glorious God better and better each day, we think you'll see your actions and attitudes are forever changed—because of who He is.

What You'll Need

A pen to record your study notes and a journal for additional notes and any bonus study work you choose to do.

A Bible. If you don't have one, we recommend investing in a good study Bible. Visit Katie's resources page at KatieOrr.me for solid study Bible suggestions.

Both a Hebrew interlinear Bible and Hebrew lexicon. There are in-print and free online versions for both. Check out my resources page for links.

A Few Important Notes

This is only one method. This approach is my attempt at distilling down how I enjoy spending time in God's Word. There are other great methods both Chris and I use from time to time. Take what you can from this method and use what works for you; make it your own.

Fifteen minutes is just the starting point. Some of us are in a stage of life where we'll take 15 minutes whenever we can get it. Others may be able to carve out more time. I will give you suggestions for how to shorten or lengthen the study as needed. I think you will find yourself looking up at the clock and realizing you've accomplished a lot in a short amount of time.

Using online study tools will be of great help. You can certainly do this study without getting online; however, you will expedite many of the processes by utilizing the powerful—and free—online tools I suggest throughout our time together. I totally get that being online while trying to connect with God has its distracting challenges. Do what works for you. There is no "right" way to do this study. The only way to "fail" is to stop meeting with God.

Resist the urge to consult commentaries and study Bible notes right away. I am thankful for all the resources we have at our fingertips, but oftentimes devotionals, study Bibles, and the latest, greatest Bible teacher can be a crutch that keeps us from learning how to walk intimately with God on our own. While I do believe there is only one true meaning of each verse, God has a personalized word to speak to each of us through this study. Receiving big news from a loved one in a deliberate and personalized way means so much more than receiving the news third-hand, and when the Holy Spirit reveals a message to our hearts through God's Word, it will be something we hold much more closely than someone else's experience of God. If at the end of the week, you are still unsure of the meaning of the passage, you can then look through commentaries.

For a list of our favorite online and print resources, including Hebrew study tools, commentaries, cross-referencing tools, and study Bibles, check out Katie's resources page at KatieOrr.me.

HOW TO FOCUS

OVER THE NEXT six weeks we will study Jonah together using the FOCUSed15 study method. Think of us as your Bible coaches. We will point you to the goal, give you what you need, and cheer you on—but you'll be the one doing the work.

In order for this study to be most helpful for group settings, we've decided to make it a six-week study. Here is where we're headed:

- **Week 1**   Jonah 1:1–6
- **Week 2**   Jonah 1:7–16
- **Week 3**   Jonah 1:17 and 2:1–10
- **Week 4**   Jonah 3
- **Week 5**   Jonah 4
- **Week 6**   The Character of God

At the end of the study we have additional study resources, including a bonus week of Bible study to help out with the cultural context of Jonah's situation. If you have the additional time available and are unfamiliar with that historical time frame, this is a great place for you to start off your study.

The FOCUSed15 method may be different from other studies you've completed. We're focusing on quality, not quantity. The goal isn't to see how quickly we can get through each verse but how deeply we can go into each verse and find everything we can about what is portrayed. This is how we can go deeper, in as little as fifteen minutes a day, by looking at the same passage over the course of several days, each day using a new lens to view it. We're not trying to get everything we can out of the passage the first time we sit in front of it. Instead, we'll come back to it again and again, peeling back each layer, fifteen minutes at a time.

The FOCUSed15 Bible Study Method

For me (Katie), high school history homework typically consisted of answering a set of questions at the end of the chapter. I quickly found that the best use of my time was to take each question, one at a time, and skim through the chapter with the question in mind. So, if the question was about Constantine, I would read the chapter wearing my "Constantine Glasses." All I looked for were facts about Constantine.

Little did I know then, this "glasses" method would become my favorite way to study God's Word. The FOCUSed15 method is essentially changing to a new pair of glasses with each read, using a different focus than the read before. Together, we will study one passage for five days, each day using a different part of the FOCUSed15 method.

- **Day 1**   Foundation: Enjoy Every Word
- **Day 2**   Observation: Look at the Details
- **Day 3**   Clarification: Uncover the Original Meaning
- **Day 4**   Utilization: Discover the Connections
- **Day 5**   Summation: Respond to God's Word

For each day in our study, I will guide you through a different lens of the FOCUSed15 study method, designed to be completed in as little as fifteen minutes a day. There are also bonus study ideas with every day, providing ways to spend more time and dig even deeper if you can. We'll pray together each day, declaring our dependence on the Spirit of God to open the eyes of our hearts to the truths in God's Word.

Foundation: Enjoy Every Word

Many of us are conditioned to read through Scripture quickly and are often left having no idea what we just read. So, to kick off our studies, we will write out our verses. Nothing too fancy, but an incredibly efficient way to slow down and pay attention to each word on the page.

Observation: Look at the Details

With our foundation work behind us, we'll spend the next day looking for truths in God's Word. This is a powerful use of our time; we cannot rightly apply the Bible to our lives if we do not accurately see what is there. Observation is simply noting what we see by asking ourselves a set of questions. We're not yet trying to figure out what it means; we are simply beginning an assessment. I will guide you along the way as we look for specific truths like, "What does this passage say is true about God?"

Clarification: Uncover the Original Meaning

This is going to be fun. We'll take a peek at the original language of the verses. Our three passages are in the New Testament, so we'll look up the original Hebrew they were written in. To do this we'll follow three simple steps:

Step 1: DECIDE which word you would like to study.

In this step, we will look for any repeated words or key words to look up, choose one, and learn more about it.

Step 2: DISCOVER that word as it was originally written.

Next, using an interlinear Bible, we'll find the original Hebrew word for the English word we chose in Step 1.

Step 3: DEFINE that word.

Finally, we will learn about the full meaning of each Hebrew word using a Hebrew lexicon, which is very much like a dictionary. We'll walk through an example together each week. You can also bookmark How to Do a Greek/Hebrew Word Study in the appendix for your reference throughout the study.

Utilization: Discover the Connections

> *The infallible rule of interpretation of Scripture is the Scripture itself: and therefore, when there is a question about the true and full sense of any Scripture . . . it must be searched and known by other places that speak more clearly.*
> —THE WESTMINSTER CONFESSION OF FAITH

Ever notice the little numbers and letters inserted in your study Bible? Most have them. The numbers are footnotes, helpful bits of information about the original text. The little letters are cross-references and important tools for study.

Cross-references do just that, referencing across the Bible where the word or phrase is used in other passages. They may also refer to a historical event or prophecy significant to the verse you are studying.

Together, we will follow a few of the cross-references for each of our passages, as they will often lead us to a better understanding of the main teaching of our verses. If your Bible doesn't have cross-references, no worries! I will provide verses for you to look up and refer you to online tools for bonus studies.

Summation—Respond to God's Word

> *A respectable acquaintance with the opinions of the giants of the past, might have saved many an erratic thinker from wild interpretations and outrageous inferences.*
> —CHARLES SPURGEON

This is when we begin to answer the question, "How should this passage affect me?" To understand this we will take three actions:

1. Identify—Find the main idea of the passage.

With a robust study of our passage accomplished, we can now do the work of interpretation. Interpretation is simply figuring out what it all means. This is oftentimes difficult to do. However, if we keep in mind the context and make good observations of the text, a solid interpretation will typically result.

This is when we will finally consult our study Bibles and commentaries! Commentaries are invaluable tools when interpreting Scripture. They are available on the entire Bible, as well as volumes on just one book of the Bible. For a list of free online commentaries, as well as in-print investments, check out KatieOrr.me/Resources.

2. Modify—Evaluate my beliefs in light of the main idea.

Once we have figured out what the passage means, we can now apply the passage to our lives. Many tend to look at application as simply finding something to change in their actions. Much in the Bible will certainly lead us to lifestyle changes, but there is another category of application we often miss: what we believe.

We must learn to see the character of God in what we study and ask ourselves how our view of Him lines up with what we see. Of course it is helpful to look for do's and don'ts to follow, but without an ever-growing knowledge of who God is, the commands become burdensome.

3. Glorify—Align my life to reflect the truth of God's Word.

When we see God for the glorious, grace-filled Savior He is, the natural response is worship; the do's and don'ts become a joy as they become a way to honor the One we love with our lives. Worship is true application.

All of This . . . in 15 Minutes?

Yes, we know this seems like a lot of ground to cover. Don't worry! We'll be here to walk you through each day. Remember, instead of trying to go as fast as we can through a passage, we are going to take it slow and intentional. We'll look at one passage for an entire week and apply one part of the method to the passage each day.

If You Have More Time . . .

We've tried to make each day's study to be around fifteen minutes of work. Because we know some days allow for more time than others, we want to give you additional assignments you can enjoy if time allows. If you complete a day and find you have some extra time, consider the "If You Have More Time . . ." portion.

The Cheat Sheet

At the end of many of the days' studies, we've included a "cheat sheet." While trying to complete a Bible study, we've found that many often find themselves paralyzed with wondering, *Am I doing this the right way?* The cheat sheet is there for you to use as a reference point. It is not a list of correct answers, however, and is meant instead to provide just a little bit of guidance here and there to let you know you are on the right track.

There are also several references in the appendix you may want to consult throughout our time together. If you are new to Bible study, you might consider spending a day to read through the appendices before beginning your study. We hope those pages will be of great help to you.

Points to Ponder

For each section of Jonah (bonus week included) I (Chris) have provided some important themes and application points for each section. We hope you'll enjoy these as a way to summarize your study, as well as hit on themes we didn't mention during the week's earlier commentary.

A Note to the Overwhelmed

Bible study is not a competition or something to achieve. It is a way of communicating with our magnificent God. If you have little time or mental capacity, ignore the bonus study ideas and enjoy what you can. Keep moving through the study each day, and know that you have taken a step of obedience to meet with God in His Word. Other seasons of life will allow for longer, deeper study. For now, embrace these precious moments in the Word and remember that Jesus is your righteousness. When God looks at you—overwhelmed and burned-out though you are—He sees the faithful obedience and perfection of Christ on your behalf, and He is pleased. Rest in that today, weary one.

WEEK 1

As believers, we cannot disobey the Lord without paying a price. Certainly our spiritual life weakens. The skills and abilities God has bestowed on us will atrophy from lack of use while we waste time fleeing.

—CHARLES STANLEY

If you long to experience peace with God, run to Him and not away from Him. He is there and wants to embrace you.

—TONY EVANS

HAVE YOU EVER thought about what your life would be like if you were on a reality television show? If you are like us you have zero desire to star in a reality show for at least two reasons. First, our lives are not interesting enough to be broadcast for others to see. Second, there is the very real possibility that others would see the most embarrassing moments of our lives. Most of us have suffered romantic rejection, failed miserably at work, put on more weight than we'd like to admit, or had our hopes and dreams crushed. However, few of us have ever had these occasions captured on camera for all posterity. As horrible as that sounds, this is essentially what we see in the Book of Jonah—a glimpse into a man's life at his worst moment.

In the opening passage of Jonah we are introduced to a man who has been called by God to a specific task. Jonah's response sets in motion one of the most unique interactions with God in all of human history. Instead of trusting God, Jonah flees the scene and is swallowed by a fish. After repenting of his faithlessness, Jonah completes the assignment but remains hostile to the people of Nineveh. As readers of this story, we may find Jonah's actions curious. It may help us to understand the context in which Jonah found himself.

If you read the optional bonus week that provides the context of Jonah's life, you learned Jonah was a prophet of Israel (2 Kings 14:25) whose ministry occurred in the 700s BC. The nation of Israel had enjoyed peace and prosperity under kings David and Solomon from 1060–1000 BC. However, in the years following King Solomon's death, the nation split into two kingdoms: Israel in the north and Judah in the south. Judah was led by several kings who loved God, but Israel never had a king who managed to follow the Lord. God sent many prophets to warn Israel of the dangers of disobedience. Jonah was one such messenger of God.

When God called Jonah to leave Israel and go to Nineveh, it was a call to minister to the enemy. Nineveh was a city in the Assyrian Empire, which was not only the major world power at the time but was also notoriously brutal. There is ancient artwork depicting Assyrians flaying their adversaries, carving flesh off the bones of living people. In fact, within a generation of Jonah's ministry the Assyrians would conquer Israel and carry off its people into captivity. In some ways, Jonah had good reason to be fearful of these people.

As you study this week, be careful not to be overly critical of Jonah. Try to place yourself in his shoes. How would you respond if God called you to go to a place where Christians suffered violence? On the other hand, make sure not to minimize the seriousness of Jonah's sin. Jonah knew what God wanted and did the exact opposite.

FOUNDATION

[FOCUSING ON JONAH 1:1–6]

You will show me the way of life, granting me the joy of your presence and the pleasures of living with you forever.

—Psalm 16:11 NLT

DOZENS OF STUDENTS sat in pews with arms crossed and heads tilted, exuding a too-cool-for-school attitude while they "listened" to the chapel service at their school. Friday after Friday, someone preached to these teenagers about being a good Christian. Count the cost. Be sold-out for God. Jesus suffered and died for you; the least you can do is live for Him.

As a teenager, I (Katie) thought counting the cost for Jesus meant throwing away my secular music and wearing a Christian T-shirt. The chapel speakers encouraged me to be "sold-out" for Jesus, but they might as well have asked me to go to jail for Jesus. Both seemed equally daunting.

I honestly thought that if I surrendered my life to God I would end up in a hut in Africa married to an ugly man. Yep. Hut. Africa. Ugly husband. Worst fate ever for a sixteen-year-old. I pictured a sold-out-for-Jesus Katie as void of all comforts, accolades, and purpose besides "living for God."

Obviously, I had a lot to learn about living for the glory of God.

Oh, how I had it all backwards! I spent years wanting more of God in my life but unsure of how to experience Him outside of youth group and Bible class. The fears of my heart paralyzed me from following the promptings of the Spirit.

Jonah had fears too. And I really can't blame him for running. I've been the runner myself. My guess is you've been too.

Sometimes our running looks just like Jonah's physical flight to Tarshish. Sometimes it looks like that sixteen-year-old girl—glued to her pew, refusing to follow the Spirit of God.

1. Before we dive into Jonah 1:1–6, spend a moment in prayer. Ask God to open your eyes to the important truths in this story.

Now it's time to start using the FOCUSed15 method of study. We'll be studying the same passage all week, which gives us a chance to pull back and look at these verses through different lenses each day.

Enjoy Every Word

2. We are going to enjoy the story of Jonah by slowly take in the setting, characters, and scenery. Read Jonah 1:1–6, and write out the story as you go along. You could write it out word-for-word, jot it down like a play, or you can summarize the main events. If you are artistic, you may enjoy drawing out each scene. There is no right or wrong way to do this. It is simply an exercise of intentionally taking in each word. We'll build on what we learn from this practice throughout the rest of the week.

3. Which words or phrases in Jonah 1:1–6 stand out to you?

4. Record any questions you have about this passage. Your questions should be answered by the end of the week, as you continue to study. If not, you'll have an opportunity to consult commentaries later.

We runners, we have trust issues. Yes, Jonah chose disobedience. Yes, I chose to sit instead of walk forward in obedience (again and again). But the issue is not in the fleeing or the sitting. It's more than our actions. Our actions (or inactions) are simply a reflection of our hearts.

Our heart's position is the problem. We refuse to trust that God is good and trustworthy. Our view of God is small and our view of self is inflated. Our reluctancy plagues our heart, binding us captive to the fear of what-ifs.

Instead of giving into fearful fleeing, we need to focus on God's faithfulness. Let's release the notion that we can control our circumstances and embrace the pursuit of the presence of God. It is only in His presence that we experience the peace, joy, and fulfillment we long for. We're praying you will experience that fulfillment this week.

{God, I confess my tendency to mistrust You. Though You are perfectly faithful and trustworthy, I listen to the whispers of the evil one, telling me You do not want what is best for me. Instead of running away from You, I want to run to You, into Your capable, strong, life-giving presence.}

IF YOU HAVE MORE TIME . . .

Foundation

For a fresh perspective, read this passage in a translation you don't often use.

Write out Jonah 2:1–2 onto a few 3-by-5 cards in your favorite translation. Keep the verses with you and/or post them up around your house. Begin committing them to memory. Each week we'll add a few more verses. The end goal will be to have Jonah 2:1–9 memorized.

If you haven't done the bonus study already, complete day 1 of the context study on page 154.

OBSERVATION

[FOCUSING ON JONAH 1:1–6]

Beloved, do not imitate evil but imitate good.

—3 John 1:11

I (CHRIS) AM an admitted procrastinator. As was often the case during my college years, I put off studying as long as I could. My go-to strategy was to look over my notes the night before the exam, and then on test day I'd feverishly study until the moment the tests were passed out.

During my junior year I was running my playbook to perfection, or so I thought. I was studying for an exam in my 3:00 p.m. class during a lecture in my 1:30 p.m. class. At least that is what I did until the professor suddenly halted her lecture and started walking my way. In a forceful tone she said, "Are you reading for another class during my lecture? How dare you?" Busted . . . or so I thought.

You see, sitting right in front of me was my roommate. Unbeknownst to me, he was also doing work for another class. The professor chewed him out in front of the whole class in a manner I will never forget. Though I was not the one who was chastised in that moment, I learned from my roommate's reaming and put my work aside.

We can all learn from the mistakes of others. In Jonah, as with many narratives in the Bible, we don't see any commands for us to follow, but there is still much to pay attention to. The lives of people that are recorded in Scripture provide attitudes and actions for us to either adopt or avoid. The Book of Jonah holds many attitudes and actions for us to consider—mostly to avoid.

1. Open your time with God through prayer, expressing your gratefulness for God's Word. Ask the Holy Spirit for His wisdom and revelation as we dive deeper into the truths held in this story.

Look at the Details

We get to put our observation glasses on today. This is another place in our study where it is easy to skip to interpretation. Just write what the text shows. We're simply gathering facts.

2. Read Jonah 1:1–6, looking for all the actions of God and Jonah.

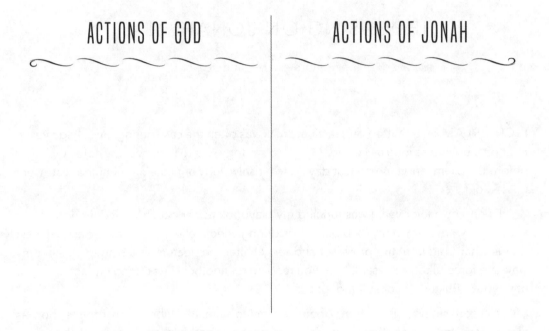

ACTIONS OF GOD

ACTIONS OF JONAH

3. Now, look back at the actions of God you've observed. What do these actions reveal about who God is?

Observing the details in Scripture is so much more than list-making. We're shaping our theology when we observe Scripture in this way; we're intentionally learning more about God, where we stand as His children, and how we are to live out God's purpose for our lives.

{*God, I'm thankful You speak to Your people. You bring encouragement, correction, and directives for our good. Make me open to hear Your voice and willing to obey Your commands. Show me where I am currently running from Your presence instead of drawing near to You.*}

IF YOU HAVE MORE TIME . . .

Observation

Note all you can learn about the mariners.

Work through the Bonus Study Week in the appendix (if you haven't already).

CLARIFICATION

[FOCUSING ON JONAH 1:1–6]

Seek the LORD and his strength; seek his presence continually!

—Psalm 105:4

IF YOU'VE NEVER seen a T-ball game, do yourself a favor and go watch one. T-ball is a great way for kids to learn the rules of a fairly complex game. Because of these complexities, the learning curve is steep, which provides many opportunities for some hilarious moments.

It can be confusing for a preschooler to remember which way to run when the ball is hit. You have two sets of coaches—and two set of fans—all consecutively yelling instructions to children on both teams. In all of the commotion, kids forget which way they are supposed to run. Sometimes a batter will run to third base instead of first. Other times a runner will skip a base, or stop mid-stride to grab their teammate's hit ball and throw it to first. Once we saw a kid hear his parents say, "Run home!" and he ran off the field to head to the car. He thought it was time to go home.

As comical as it is to watch these cuties run the wrong way in T-ball, it is not nearly as funny to watch people run the wrong way in life. In our study this week, we watch Jonah run the wrong way because he believes he can outrun the presence of God. Jonah's fundamental misunderstanding of God's presence cost him dearly.

1. Open today's time with a prayer. Ask God to open the eyes of your heart to see the fallacies you believe about God. Declare your desire to seek His presence, instead of run from it.

Uncover the Original Meaning

As part of our Clarification day, we come to our Hebrew study. You may be a bit intimidated by the thought of studying the original language, but it's an important layer we get to peel back. With the right tools, studying the Hebrew can be as simple as looking up a word in the dictionary. If this is your first attempt at Hebrew study or you need a refresher, I encourage you to check out the videos I (Katie) have created to show you how to use many of the online Hebrew tools. Just head to KatieOrr.me/Resources, and look for the VIDEOS section.

DECIDE which word you would like to study.

2. To start your Hebrew study, look for any potential key words in Jonah 1:1–6. As you find any repeated word or words that seem important to the passage, write them down below.

You may have noticed that the word *presence* is used multiple times. Let's start there.

DISCOVER that word as it was originally written.

Now that you know what you want to study, you need to look up the word *presence* to find out what the original Hebrew word is. An interlinear Bible will show you English verses and line up each word next to the Hebrew words they were translated from. You can find these tools in print form, but the easiest way to use them is through the many free online websites and/or smart phone applications I've listed on my website. Many of these resources will make this step easy. You can find the Hebrew word with a click of a button or tap of the screen.

3. Using your preferred tool, see if you can find the original word for *presence*, and write it below.

For a more detailed explanation of what is going on behind the scenes of your app or website tool, check out How to Do a Greek/Hebrew Word Study in the appendix.

DEFINE that word.

Now that you know the original word for *presence* used in verse 3 is *paneh*, we can look up this Hebrew word to better define and uncover the original meaning. For this, we will fill out the following chart.

HEBREW WORD:
paneh

VERSE AND VERSION:
Jonah 1:3 ESV

Part of Speech:
(verb, noun, etc.)

noun

Translation Notes:
(How else is it translated? How often is this word used?)

used 1,947 times; also translated into: before, face, front (and many more)

Strong's Concordance Number:
H6440

Definition:
front, head, face

Notes:
94 times of 1,947 translated as "presence" (in ESV), translated into "before" 1,008 times of 1,947

4. Now, why don't you try it on your own? Use the above steps to look up the word *thought* in verse 6, and fill in the chart provided. (If you are brand new to Bible study this may be overwhelming. That's OK. It was for me, as well. Just give it a try, and if you're not up for looking up Hebrew, choose a few words to look up in the dictionary and write out their definitions. This is still a great way to do our Clarification work of better understanding the meaning of each word.)

HEBREW WORD: VERSE AND VERSION:

Part of Speech:
(verb, noun, etc.)

Translation Notes:
(How else is it translated? How often is this word used?)

Strong's Concordance Number:

Definition:

Notes:

Sometimes life is overwhelming, and when we hear the call of God, whether it be a specific directive or a general call to His ways over ours, we have a choice just as Jonah did. We can run toward God or attempt to flee His presence. The thing most of us forget in these overwhelming moments is this: only God has what we need. Only His presence brings peace, joy, power, and victory. As we seek His presence, we are strengthened for the call. Jonah missed this. We often miss this too.

{God, give me a resolve to follow You wherever You lead me. Help me to remember in my overwhelmed moments that You are good, powerful, and will provide everything I need to follow You in obedience.}

IF YOU HAVE MORE TIME . . .

Clarification

Follow the Hebrew study steps for additional words in Jonah 1:1–6. Check out the resource library at KatieOrr.me/Resources for a blank Hebrew worksheet.

Work through the Bonus Study Week in the appendix (if you haven't already).

UTILIZATION

[FOCUSING ON JONAH 1:1–6]

My son, do not despise the LORD's discipline or be weary of his reproof, for the LORD reproves him whom he loves, as a father the son in whom he delights.

—Proverbs 3:11–12

IMAGINE A WORLD where the correction of wrong actions and attitudes are always withheld. If you really think about it, this scenario is terrifying. Cars, buildings, and airplanes would be death traps because their designers never correct any flaws. Food would be unsafe because its manufacturers never adjust course, even if poison is introduced into the food supply. Computers and technology would never operate as advertised because the bugs would never be worked out.

No one likes to be corrected, but living in a world without correction is not an option. Correction is necessary for growth, progress, and safety. Correction, though, is about concern for the one who is out of line. We see this most clearly in parenting a young child. Only the most unloving parent refuses to correct a child facing danger. If a child you love is playing in traffic, your natural response is correction. Withholding correction, in this case, would be equal to hatred.

Over and over in the Book of Jonah, we see the corrective hand of God. Just like a loving parent, our Heavenly Father brings needed correction into Jonah's life—not out of condemnation but out of love.

1. Spend a few moments thanking God for His gracious hand of correction.

Discover the Connections

2. Read Jonah 1:1–6 to start your study.

It's time for our Utilization study, where we'll simply look up verses related to any word or phrase we want to learn more about. To do this, you can use the cross-referencing letters in your study Bible or online study tools. You can also use a Bible dictionary to look up people, places, and themes in the Bible. If your Bible doesn't have cross references, no worries. There are many free online tools and smart phone apps. Check out the resources page at KatieOrr.me/Resources for a list of cross-referencing tools. Plus, I'll always start you out with a few suggestions for your study.

3. Look up each of the following references, and take notes of any truths that reveal a bigger picture of the threads this verse is attached to. You might consider applying one or more of the FOCUS method steps to that passage, depending on the time you have for the day. I typically enjoy listing out truths I see, especially those that help me understand the original passage I'm studying. You can write out the passage in the space provided or even look up a Hebrew word or two in your interlinear Bible. Just do what interests you and what you have time for! There are additional reference ideas in the bonus study section at the beginning of this week's study.

come up before me (v. 2)

Genesis 18:20–21

Ezra 9:6

Revelation 18:5

away from the presence of the Lord (v. 3)

Genesis 4:16

Psalm 139:9–10

As a holy sovereign and judge, God will not be in the presence of sin. Justice must be served. Sin must be punished. This is why the life, death, and resurrection of Christ is such good news. His perfect life was enough to appease the debt our sin created. Through a relationship with Christ, where He becomes our righteousness, we can now enter into the holy presence of God without fear of judgment.

{God, my sin is great. I am so thankful for the way You created through Christ so that I can enjoy Your presence for eternity. Help me remember that I can run to You—even in my worst moments. You are waiting with open arms, full of grace.}

IF YOU HAVE MORE TIME . . .

Utilization

Look up the following cross references and any additional words and/or phrases in this week's passage you would like to learn more about.

the LORD hurled a great wind upon the sea (v. 4)

Psalm 107:25

Psalm 147:15–18

Psalm 148:7–8

each cried out to his god (v. 5)

Psalm 107:6, 13, 19, 28

Work through the Bonus Study Week in the appendix (if you haven't already).

SUMMATION

[FOCUSING ON JONAH 1:1–6]

Where shall I go from your Spirit? Or where shall I flee from your presence?

—Psalm 139:7

DON'T YOU HATE it when a plan backfires? The words you meant to be comforting turn out to hurt a friend's feelings. The software update you thought would make your device run faster actually slows it down. The money-saving measure you take costs you more. We have all had those times when what we fear happens despite our best efforts to avoid it.

In Jonah 1, we see the prophet's plan backfire in extraordinary fashion. Jonah fears the Ninevites. He is afraid that if he goes to them they will reject his message and harm him, or accept his message and receive God's mercy. Jonah would like to avoid both of these outcomes. By running from God's assignment Jonah finds himself in danger anyway.

Anytime we seek to run from God's call we are not running away from danger but into it. Jonah believed he could choose to find safety on his own, rather than surrender to God's will.

1. Ask God to continue His work in your heart. Invite Him to search your heart and reveal any places that need changing.

Respond to God's Word

Today, let's take some time to slow down and digest what we've been learning by going through our Summation steps. Remember, this is when we begin to answer the question, "How should what I've learned affect me?"

IDENTIFY—Find the main idea of each passage.

2. Take a few moments to flip back to each day's study to review what you've learned this week. In the space provided, write out Jonah 1:1–6 in your own words. Or simply write out what you think the main idea of the passage is.

3. Read a commentary or study Bible to see how your observations from this week line up with the scholars. (You can find links to free online commentary options as well as in-print investment suggestions for your library at KatieOrr.me/Resources.) As you search commentaries, ask God to make clear the meaning of any passages that are fuzzy to you. Record any additional observations below.

MODIFY—Evaluate my beliefs in light of the main idea.

Journal prayerfully through the following questions, asking the Spirit of God to enlighten and convict.

4. Do my attitudes and actions resemble Jonah's rebellion in any way?

5. Are my words consistent with my actions? If I say I trust and serve God, do my actions match that declaration?

6. What is my attitude toward surrendering all for God's purposes and glory?

Completely Afraid
of Surrender

Experiencing the Joy and
Freedom of Surrender

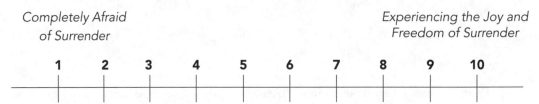

7. What is my attitude toward correction from God?

Despise Receiving
Correction

Welcome the
Needed Redirecting

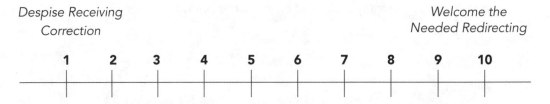

GLORIFY—Align my life to reflect the truth of God's Word.

8. What situations am I currently struggling to trust God with and walk forward in obedience? (Consider asking a friend, spouse, and/or trusted mentor to pray for you in regards to this situation.)

9. What can I do this week to remind myself of God's goodness, trustworthiness, and sovereignty? (Some examples we enjoy: writing out verses to hang up around your home, taking some time to journal and/or pray and praise God for His past faithfulness in your life, intentionally spending time with a friend who will point you to God's goodness.)

{God, I am grateful for Your patience with me. I am more like Jonah than I care to admit. I shirk responsibility, forget that my life is not all about me, and ignore the reality of the lost. Holy Spirit, stir up in me a great awareness of Your work in and around me. By Your grace, I choose to walk forward in obedience and run to You, instead of away from You.}

IF YOU HAVE MORE TIME . . .

Summation

Spend additional time in commentaries.

Add a title to this section in your outline in the appendix on page 174.

Grab your journal and continue the conversation with God about what He is teaching you.

Share what you are learning with a trusted friend. Ask them to pray for you as you apply what you've learned.

Work through the Bonus Study Week in the appendix (if you haven't already).

WEEK 1: POINTS TO PONDER

[FOCUSING ON JONAH 1:1–6]

Our actions reveal our true beliefs.

BY ATTEMPTING TO run away from God's assignment, Jonah was essentially trying to run from God. It was a common belief in Jonah's time that gods were merely regional deities, meaning gods were bound to a small geographic area or people. This was the view of the sailors who all cried out to their own gods (v. 5). Jonah may have known Yahweh was the one true God, but his actions indicate he was more like the sailors than he would care to admit.

God doesn't always immediately intervene.

Jonah most likely lived inland. We are told in verse three that Jonah went down to Joppa. Down does not refer to heading south on the map. This indicates going down in altitude, from higher elevations, which is what we find inland to the west of the Jordan River. This is relevant because it was a long walk from the mountainous plain of central Israel to the coast of the Mediterranean Sea at Joppa. If God wanted to stop Jonah He certainly could have done so before Jonah left town.

Disobedience is the opposite of obedience.

Tell me something I don't know, right? Tarshish was west of Israel, Nineveh was to the east. Jonah was not taking the scenic route; he was running as fast as he could in the opposite direction. Sin is always the opposite of going God's way.

Nothing happens by chance.

We are told in verse 4 that God hurled the wind onto the sea. This was no coincidental storm; it was the hand of God moving against Jonah. Our God is a God of details and is intricately acquainted with every moment of our lives.

You can't fix spiritual problems by physical means.

In verse 5 the sailors respond to the storm by jettisoning cargo from the ship. While this makes sense physically, it does not address the real problem—God was against them. No matter how much cargo they threw over the side of the boat, God was not going to relent until Jonah learned the lesson. The issue was not a buoyancy problem but a sin problem. We can't fix our sin problem by physical means either. No amount of washing, giving, or serving can ever fix the problem caused by our sin. Only Jesus can fix our sin problem.

Hard hearts fail to honor God in many ways.

Not only was Jonah running from his assignment, he wasn't even attempting to minister to the crew. If anything you might think Jonah would try to start a ministry effort on the boat to make the point that many people are in need of God's mercy. However, Jonah demonstrates no such desire and is asleep when the storm hits. It is the sailors who have to remind Jonah to pray in the midst of that storm. If our hearts are hard toward God, this will usually come out in many areas of our lives.

WEEK 1: CHEAT SHEET

Day 2: Observation

2. Read Jonah 1:1–6, looking for all the actions of God and Jonah.

ACTIONS OF GOD	ACTIONS OF JONAH
Sent a word to Jonah (v. 1)	Ran from the Lord, to Joppa, in opposite direction of what he was told (v. 3)
Commissioned Jonah to bring a warning (v. 2)	Hired a ship to take him to Tarshish (v. 3)
Hurled a great wind on the sea that threatened to break up the ship (v. 4)	

3. Now, look back at the actions of God you've observed. What do these actions reveal about who God is?

– God is a merciful God. He brings warning to those who are perishing.

– God speaks to His people.

– God uses people to carry out His work. He chooses to use us in His great redemptive plan.

– God commands and controls the sea.

Day 3: Clarification

4. Now, why don't you try it on your own? Use the above steps to look up the word *thought* in verse 6, and fill in the chart provided.

HEWBREW WORD:
ashath

VERSE AND VERSION:
Jonah 1:6 ESV

Part of Speech:
(verb, noun, etc.)

verb

Translation Notes:
(How else is it translated? How often is this word used?)

Used two times; also translated as "shine"

Strong's Concordance Number:
H6245

Definition:
to recollect, to recall to mind

Notes:

act. favorably, formally, take notice, remember, or think about, i.e., deliver someone from danger as a figurative extension of a person seeing and responding to a situation [James Swanson, Dictionary of Biblical Languages with Semantic Domains: Hebrew (Old Testament). Oak Harbor: Logos Research Systems, Inc., 1997.]

WEEK 2

His timing is perfect. His will is our hiding place. Lord Jesus, keep me in Your will! Don't let me go mad by poking about outside it.

—CORRIE TEN BOOM, *THE HIDING PLACE*

The only fear I have is to fear to get out of the will of God. Outside of the will of God, there's nothing I want, and in the will of God there's nothing I fear, for God has sworn to keep me in His will. If I'm out of His will, that is another matter. But if I'm in His will, He's sworn to keep me.

—A. W. TOZER, *SUCCESS AND THE CHRISTIAN*

WHO KNEW A purple dress could elicit such fear? When I (Chris) was in the sixth grade there was an administrator at my school; we'll call her Mrs. G. This lady stood no more than five feet tall and always wore purple clothes. Always. Every . . . single . . . day. Purple and white were the school colors, but I cannot confirm if this had anything to do with her wardrobe decisions. In hindsight, perhaps she was a bit odd.

In any case, my run in with this middle school administrator is one I'll never forget. One day I was sent by my teacher to Mrs. G's office for disciplinary reasons. I remember the terror as I listened on a speaker phone to this diminutive woman discuss disciplinary options with my mother. I don't remember what course of action we ultimately decided on but I do recall this woman threatened to take away baseball.

This encounter left my professional sports career in jeopardy. All of this was deeply distressing to me because I was a child who did not get in much trouble. Being overwhelmed by the intensity of the situation, and not knowing what else to do, I cried my eyes out that day.

Oh, you're probably wondering what atrocity I committed to deserve this particular intervention. The act in question was my failure to bring a calculator to science class. As ludicrous as it may seem to put a child through this because of a calculator, there was a lesson to be learned: rules are rules, and the cost of disobedience is steep. In the section we will be studying this week, Jonah learned the cost of his rebellion against God.

After receiving the call from God to go to Nineveh, Jonah runs the opposite direction. Last week we saw some of the motivating factors that caused Jonah to flee. This week we will begin to see the fallout of Jonah's sin. The faithless prophet's rebellion brings about a storm. This storm costs the sailors their cargo and potentially their lives. It is only after Jonah is tossed overboard that they are removed from danger.

During the course of your study time try and put yourself into the story. Look at it from Jonah's perspective. Look again from the view of the crew. Would you have done anything differently, or would you have done the same? We're praying for your time in Jonah this week!

FOUNDATION

[FOCUSING ON JONAH 1:7–16]

God called the dry land Earth, and the waters that were gathered together he called Seas. And God saw that it was good.

—Genesis 1:10

IF YOU ASK most people to name a famous composer they will probably say Beethoven or Mozart. These musical geniuses created some of the most important and iconic music in the history of the world. You don't have to know much about music theory to know that Mozart's Fortieth and Beethoven's Ninth Symphonies are masterpieces.

The thing about music composition is that although it involves a composer and musical symbols (notes, rests, time signatures, etc.), it is not a collaboration between the composer and those symbols. Beethoven never wrote a B-flat that turned around and argued with him. Mozart never inserted a quarter rest that questioned his decision.

The beauty in a symphony does not come from the teamwork of a composer and his musical notations; beauty comes from the complete mastery of the composer over his notations. In the same way, God does not collaborate with nature. God commands nature.

1. Before we dive into Jonah 1:7–16, spend a moment in prayer. Ask God to open your eyes to the life-changing truths in this passage.

Enjoy Every Word

2. Once again, for our Foundation day, we'll work through the first layer of this week's section of Jonah 1:7–16. Write out the passage below. Remember, you can also draw it out, summarize the main events, or rewrite it into scenes of a play; do whatever works for you.

3. Which words or phrases in Jonah 1:7–16 stand out to you?

4. Record any questions you have about this passage.

Our Creator is in complete control. Though the storms around us rage, we can be comforted and assured that we are always safe in His capable hands.

{God, though I sometimes act otherwise, I'm glad You are in charge. You are a perfect ruler. Holy and just, Your ways are higher than mine. I praise You for Your power and ability to command the winds and seas.}

IF YOU HAVE MORE TIME . . .

Foundation

Read Jonah 1:7–16 in a different translation.

Add Jonah 2:3–4 to your 3-by-5 cards in your favorite translation. Keep the verses with you and/or post them up around your house. Begin committing them to memory.

OBSERVATION

[FOCUSING ON JONAH 1:7–16]

The lot is cast into the lap, but its every decision is from the LORD.

—Proverbs 16:33

THERE ARE MANY methods we can use when making a decision. We can make a list of pros and cons, go with our gut, or leave it to chance by flipping a coin, drawing straws, or playing the classic rock-paper-scissors.

In each of these scenarios the person or persons needing to make a decision take a more passive approach to making a decision. As people of the Christian faith, we understand there is no such thing as chance. God is always at work in our lives. The coin will always land how God wants it to land. This is not to say that flipping a coin will always lead to the best result. Perhaps God allows the coin to land on tails to teach us to use a better technique than coin flipping!

The sailors of Jonah's day were not much different from us when it comes to decision making. They cast lots to determine the source of the trouble, and the lot fell exactly as God intended. The point of this passage is not to learn how to properly cast lots, it is to learn to trust that God can, and will, bring His plans to pass—by whatever means necessary.

1. Spend a few moments thanking God for His sovereign control over all things.

Look at the Details

2. Read Jonah 1:7–16, looking for any notable attitudes and actions displayed by Jonah. Pay special attention to any that should be avoided or adopted.

ATTITUDES AND ACTIONS OF JONAH

3. Read through Jonah 1:7–16 once more. This time note the attitudes and actions of the mariners.

ATTITUDES AND ACTIONS OF THE MARINERS

The way we live our lives matters. The eyes of the world are upon us, whether we realize it or not. The lady at the checkout counter, the mailman, our coworkers and neighbors, and every other soul we encounter has a desperate need for the rescue only our God can provide. Many, like the mariners, reach out to other gods in attempts to find peace from the storms they are facing. Yet only a saving faith in God will bring deliverance from their greatest foe—sin. And the Christians around them must be ready and willing to share the hope they have in Christ. If we are tied up in our own disobedient living, we will not be found as a beacon of light to those around us. May our lives be ones of integrity and readiness, not hypocrisy and rebellion.

{God, I long for my life to be used by You to bring those who do not know You into a relationship with You. Help me to better see the disobedient ways in my life and how they affect my witness. Make me a better representative of who You are.}

IF YOU HAVE MORE TIME . . .

Observation

Look for the hand of God in the events recorded in Jonah 1:7–16. Record them in your journal.

CLARIFICATION

[FOCUSING ON JONAH 1:7–16]

The fear of the LORD is the beginning of knowledge; fools despise wisdom and instruction.

—Proverbs 1:7

OUR BOYS SHARE a bedroom. This makes bedtime somewhat of an adventure. Just because we are eager for them to be asleep doesn't mean they are ready to go to sleep. Often, we will hear chatter and giggles from their room well after lights-out. Usually a word of reminder from Dad is all that is needed get the point across. However, every now and then, a more direct method is required. The boys' reaction the moment the door slings open is very telling. If, in that moment, giggling turns to silence, we know they have a healthy amount of fear of what's to come if they continue their bedtime shenanigans.

The Bible often speaks of the fear of the Lord. Many have pointed out that this does not mean believers should be afraid of God and have suggested this word has the connotation of respect. We must be careful, though. While respect is connected to biblical fear that is not the whole story. To fear God is to rightly understand our sinfulness and His holiness. It is also to believe so strongly in God's character that it changes how we live.

If we live as though God has no bearing on the choices we make day to day, we have no fear of Him, regardless of how much we claim to respect Him.

1. Begin with a prayer declaring your desire to follow after God with a healthy amount of fear—respect and understanding—of His holiness and grandeur.

Uncover the Original Meaning

We're back again at the original Hebrew. I know this day can seem daunting and difficult, especially if this is a new skill for you. Just as learning to ride a bike or figuring out the latest technology can be frustrating at times, the rewards of leaning in and continuing on are worth it! If the thought of studying the Hebrew is still too much today, consider selecting a few words to look up in the dictionary, then rewrite the verse with the definition in place of the word you looked up. Do what works for you, but do try something!

DECIDE which word you would like to study.

2. To start your Hebrew study, look for any potential key words in Jonah 1:7–16. As you find any repeated word or words that seem important to the passage, write them down.

DISCOVER that word as it was originally written.

3. Let's discover the original word for *fear* in verse 9. When you find the Hebrew word, write it below.

DEFINE that word.

4. Fill in the Hebrew chart for the original word you found for *fear*.

HEBREW WORD: VERSE AND VERSION:

Part of Speech:
(verb, noun, etc.)

Translation Notes:
(How else is it translated? How often is this word used?)

Strong's Concordance Number:

Definition:

Notes:

5. Choose a word from your DECIDE list, and follow the rest of the Hebrew study steps to learn more about that word.

HEBREW WORD: VERSE AND VERSION:

Part of Speech:
(verb, noun, etc.)

Translation Notes:
(How else is it translated? How often is this word used?)

Strong's Concordance Number:

Definition:

Notes:

Though the mariners were caught up in the negative repercussions of Jonah's disobedience, they also experienced the power and deliverance of God. Even when we choose defiance, God can use our mess to lead others to Him.

{Lord, I am thankful You are always in control, even when I'm in the middle of messing things up. Nothing throws You, not even my willful choices of disobedience. Your plan cannot be thwarted. Your mercy cannot be spent.}

IF YOU HAVE MORE TIME . . .

Clarification
Follow the Hebrew study steps for additional words in Jonah 1:7–16. Here are a few you might start with:

afraid (v. 10)

called out (v. 14)

perish (v. 14)

WEEK 2 | DAY 4

UTILIZATION

[FOCUSING ON JONAH 1:7–16]

The Lord is not slow to fulfill his promise as some count slowness, but is patient toward you, not wishing that any should perish, but that all should reach repentance.

—2 Peter 3:9

THE PHARMACEUTICAL INDUSTRY is a massive contributor to the United States' economy. You can hardly watch television for any length of time without seeing an advertisement for a medication. At the end of every commercial the announcer quickly reads off the list of side effects. The reality is that all medication has side effects. To expect none betrays a lack of understanding of the trade off you get with medication. Usually the compromise is acceptable. I (Chris) will take a little dry mouth if it cures the bacterial infection. Other times the danger is not worth the benefit; I'd rather not have a heart attack to avoid a headache.

Sin works in much the same way; it always comes with side effects. The great lie of temptation is that we can sin without it negatively affecting us. This lie's twin is the belief that we can sin without hurting others. Both of these distortions come from the father of lies. A pastor's sin will affect his family, as well as his church. A father's sin will absolutely affect his wife and children, at a minimum. In our passage today we will see how Jonah's sin affects others.

1. Ask the Spirit of God to continue His work of gentle conviction of the sin in your life. Commit to repentance, and turn from that sin.

Discover the Connections

2. Read Jonah 1:7–16 once more to start your study.

3. Look up each of the following verses to see the threads throughout Scripture.

for you, O LORD have done as it pleased you (v. 14)

Psalm 115:3

Psalm 135:6

Daniel 4:35

the sea ceased from its raging (v. 15)

Psalm 65:5–8

Luke 8:22–24

Our God is a mighty God and our lives are to be a reflection of His loving, faithful, generous, and holy character. When we walk away from this job of mirroring Christ to those around us, they will suffer the consequences of our sins (just as we often suffer from the negative effects of the sins of others). Conversely, as we chose to walk in obedient worship and follow the ways of our Lord and Savior, others can benefit from seeing the glory of Christ in us.

{God, I do want to be a mirror of Your glory. Let it not be that others would be caught up in the storms of my sin, to their detriment. Make me a holy image of Your Son in order to bring many into a relationship with You as a result of Your work in me.}

IF YOU HAVE MORE TIME . . .

Utilization

Look up the following cross references and any additional words and/or phrases in this week's passage you would like to learn more about.

who made the sea and the dry land (v. 9)

Genesis 1:6–10

Exodus 20:11

Psalm 146:5–7

SUMMATION

[FOCUSING ON JONAH 1:7–16]

Search me, O God, and know my heart! Try me and know my thoughts! And see if there be any grievous way in me, and lead me in the way everlasting!

—Psalm 139:23–24

THE OTHER DAY we were rushing to get out the door. We had one child going to soccer and another to baseball, and time was running out to get either there at the right rime. I (Chris) asked our oldest son to find a backpack I could use to hold my stuff as I ran back and forth between sports fields. I thought this was a simple task and could not figure out why he was not getting the object I was asking for.

I didn't want him to empty one of the kid's school backpacks, so I told him to get one of those drawstring backpacks that they hand out with corporate logos at conferences. Every time he arrived with the wrong item, I kept getting more irritated. He kept insisting he was bringing me what I wanted. Finally, out of exasperation I yelled, "Get me a zipper backpack!"

That was when it hit me. Every time I thought I was saying "drawstring" I was really saying "zipper." You see, I knew what I meant, but my words did not line up with what I really wanted.

In the passage today we will see that what Jonah says does not line up with what Jonah really wants. While he says he fears the Lord, his actions indicate he does not.

Respond to God's Word

1. Ask God to move your heart to application. Commit yourself anew to following the Spirit's leading through deliberate, obedient actions.

IDENTIFY—Find the main idea of each passage.

2. Take a few moments to flip back to each day's study to review what you've learned this week. In the space below, write out Jonah 1:7–16 in your own words. Or write out what you think the main idea of the passage is.

3. Read a commentary or study Bible to see how your observations from this week line up with the scholars.

MODIFY—Evaluate my beliefs in light of the main idea.

Journal prayerfully through the following questions, asking the Spirit of God to enlighten and convict.

4. How confident am I in God's ability to lead and instruct me when I don't know what to do?

Not at All
Confident

Completely
Confident

1	2	3	4	5	6	7	8	9	10

5. What keeps me from truly fearing God?

6. What is my view of God's control over all things?

He Is an Impotent
and Distant Deity

He Is a Powerful, All-
Knowing Sovereign

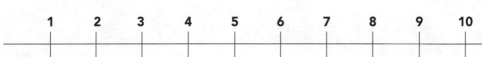

   1   2   3   4   5   6   7   8   9   10

7. How does my view of God line up with what I've learned about Him in Jonah so far?

GLORIFY—Align my life to reflect the truth of God's Word.

8. Spend some time in prayer, asking God's Spirit to conform your mind to the truths of His Word, especially about who He is.

{Lord, You are powerful, able, and personal. You can name each grain of sand, every star in the sky, as well as the hairs on my head. You are intimately acquainted with my ways. Forgive me for allowing myself to believe You are distant and disinterested in my days. Help me remember—especially when I am frightened and uncertain of the future—that You are always in control, and You always have a good plan for my life. I surrender this day to Your purposes and plan.}

IF YOU HAVE MORE TIME . . .

Summation

Spend additional time in commentaries.

Add a title to this section in your outline in the appendix on page 174.

Grab your journal and continue the conversation with God about what He is teaching you.

Share what you are learning with a trusted friend. Ask them to pray for you as you apply what you've learned.

WEEK 2: POINTS TO PONDER

[FOCUSING ON JONAH 1:7–16]

God's will was discovered after investigation.

GOD IS NOT hiding His intentions from people. If you want to know what God is up to, look to what He has said. God told Jonah His will, and God has told us His will in Scripture. We may not ever know all of the fine details of how God's plan will unfold, but we are given plenty to go on in the Bible.

The sailors were honorable men who did everything they could to keep Jonah safe.

They worked hard to row against the storm. In many ways these mariners are more honorable than Jonah. The faithless prophet put their lives in jeopardy because of his sin, whereas the unbelieving sailors put their lives in jeopardy to save his. However, this leads us to the sobering reality that honorable men go to hell without the gospel. These crewmen were honorable despite being ignorant of the one true God. In the same way we can encounter people today who are honorable, trustworthy, hardworking people. If they are ignorant or unresponsive to God's message of salvation they too will end up separated from God for eternity.

Most lessons we learn require humility.

Jonah did not jump into the sea; he was hurled. It was probably humiliating for a grown man to be thrown overboard by other men. The indignity that Jonah suffered helped drive home the point that rebellion against God will not be tolerated.

Never mistake God's patience with sinners as His tolerance of sin.

God finally begins teaching Jonah the lesson once the boat is out to sea. God could have intervened sooner, but the lesson may not have been as memorable for Jonah or us. God rarely metes out immediate correction for our sin. However, we should not fall into the error of believing God neither sees nor cares about our sin. God's kindness and patience are meant to bring us to repentance (Romans 2:4).

Our sin usually affects others.

Jonah's flight to Tarshish embroiled the entire sailing vessel into his problems. Many lives were put at risk because of Jonah's disobedience. This is often the case when we sin. This rebellion is rarely self-contained and often spills out into the lives of others.

God will use us for His glory . . . one way or another.

Jonah's refusal to minister to these sailors robbed them of an opportunity to hear the truth. It also robbed Jonah of an opportunity to bring glory to God. Fortunately for the mariners they were introduced to God through His handling of Jonah. If we will not honor God with our obedience He may use us as a negative example to others.

Read the Bible in context.

In this book, the Bible reports that Jonah is swallowed by a fish. Often when people talk about the story they say it was a whale that swallowed Jonah. The main reason for the whale theory is that it is large enough to swallow a man. The problem, according to some, is that whales aren't fish; they are mammals. If it was indeed a whale, the Bible—they say—misidentifies whales as fish and is in error. This is where context helps. During the time of Jonah they did not draw a distinction between fish and aquatic mammals. There was no verbiage to draw such a line. To expect the Bible to use modern taxonomic language would have been anachronistic. It could have been a whale or a fish, we aren't told a species. In either case, don't get hung up on the Bible's designation of the animal as a fish. Using this word in this way does not harm the Bible's reputation.

Read the Bible as its original audience would have understood it.

One of the most common questions about this book is, "Was this a real event or a fictional story?" Proponents of the fiction theory like this interpretation because it is hard to believe a fish could swallow a man and the man could survive for three days. The problem with this understanding is that the original audience of this book believed it was a real event. Sometimes the Bible does use fiction to communicate deeper truths (the parables of Jesus, for example). However, in those cases the biblical authors clearly indicated they intended to communicate fiction rather than history. Nothing in the story of Jonah gives this indication. If this was not a historical event, why use a real, historical person who goes to a real, historical city? If our only reason to reject the historicity of Jonah is to escape the supernatural components then we will also find major problems with the rest of Christianity. If there is nothing supernatural, there is no virgin birth, resurrection, no Christianity, and no God.

Be careful extrapolating God's will in natural events.

God does use nature to accomplish His purposes, but we are historically very bad at applying this truth. For example, some Christians believed Hurricane Katrina was a reaction against the sinfulness of the city of New Orleans. No doubt that town has its share of debauchery, but to interpret Hurricane Katrina as an act condemnation or judgment requires us to ignore the fact that natural disasters affect a broad swath of people, many who may not need any kind of earthly "judgment."

The point is that we cannot always understand God's reasoning, and to assume we do can lead us astray in our thinking. We must remember that while God can use nature to accomplish His good and perfect plan, sometimes even as condemnation, we must use caution when thinking about underlying causes of natural disasters (see Luke 13:1–5). God has reasons, but we may not know those reasons on this side of eternity.

WEEK 2: CHEAT SHEET

Day 2: Observation

2. Read Jonah 1:7–16, looking for any notable attitudes and actions displayed by Jonah. Pay special attention to any that should be avoided or adopted.

ATTITUDES AND ACTIONS OF JONAH

Jonah's words and actions were inconsistent. He claimed to fear God (v. 9), but his disregard for God's call on his life showed otherwise.

He chose flagrant rebellion over obedience ("For the men knew that he was fleeing from the presence of the LORD, because he had told them" v. 10). He wasn't even trying to hide his choice to run.

After realizing the danger he had brought on the mariners, Jonah showed some sort of compassion for them (or at least, decency), to be thrown into the sea on their behalf (v. 12).

3. Read through Jonah 1:7–16 once more. This time note the attitudes and actions of the mariners.

ATTITUDES AND ACTIONS OF THE MARINERS

Not sure what to do, they cast lots in order to move forward, instead of inaction (v. 7).

The mariners, though they barely knew this new-to-them God, prayed to Him and attempted "imperfect" obedience, even when they were uncertain of what exactly to do (v. 14).

The mariners responded with a healthy fear and submission of God after seeing evidence that He is the creator—and stopper—of the great storm (v. 16).

Day 3: Clarification

4. Fill in the Hebrew chart for the original word you found for *fear*.

HEBREW WORD:
yare

VERSE AND VERSION:
Jonah 1:9 ESV

Part of Speech:
(verb, noun, etc.)

adjective

Translation Notes:
(How else is it translated? How often is this word used?)

used 65 times in Old Testament, mostly translated into "fear"

Strong's Concordance Number:

H3373

Definition:

in fear of; fearful

Notes:

fear, obj. God, i.e. shudder at, be in awe of, hold in deference

WEEK 3

FOCUSING ON
JONAH 1:17 AND 2:1–10

Suffering is unbearable if you aren't certain that God is for you and with you.
—TIM KELLER, *WALKING WITH GOD THROUGH PAIN AND SUFFERING*

But pain insists upon being attended to. God whispers to us in our pleasures, speaks in our conscience, but shouts in our pain: it is His megaphone to rouse a deaf world.
—C. S. LEWIS, *THE PROBLEM OF PAIN*

MENTIONING DE LEON Springs to most residents of Central Florida will elicit fond memories. The naturally occurring spring is located just a few miles from my (Chris's) childhood home. Once inside the state park, visitors can experience the serene beauty of Florida live oak trees strewn with Spanish moss, enjoy world famous pancakes at the Sugar Mill restaurant, walk on nature trails, enjoy a family reunion on the picnic tables, and go for a swim in the springs.

For me, De Leon Springs brings to mind a distinctly different memory. As a teen, I was once dared by a friend to touch the bottom of the springs. The source of the spring lies some thirty feet below the surface. Wanting to defend my honor, I accepted the challenge and made several attempts to reach the bottom. With every failed attempt my competitive drive found a new gear. Finally, I mustered all of the courage I could find and set out to retrieve some sand, rock, or anything to prove I had indeed reached the bottom. As I swam down, I suddenly recalled all the childhood stories I had heard of divers who got trapped in the caves under the spring and died. All of this whirled around my head as I neared the bottom. Nearing the limits of my lungs capacity, I kicked the last few strokes

67

and finally reached my destination. The problem was that once on the bottom I had no more breath and still had to travel the same distance to the surface as I did on the way down. I was sure I would be added to the lore of those who never made it back up out of the water—some cautionary tale told to children for generations to come.

However, I did resurface, but not without a newfound appreciation for air and an improved fondness for dry ground. At the bottom of De Leon Springs I believe I experienced something similar to Jonah. It was frightening, for sure. As you read the passage this week you will notice Jonah's thoughts as he descends into a watery abyss. You will hear his account of sinking into the deep, assured he would die by drowning. You will also hear his prayers from the depths as he calls out to God for mercy and deliverance.

FOUNDATION

[FOCUSING ON JONAH 1:17 AND 2:1–10]

I cried aloud to the Lᴏʀᴅ, and he answered me from his holy hill.

—Psalm 3:4

IN FOOTBALL THERE is a play that every team, on every level, practices but hopes they never have to use. The play is known as the Hail Mary pass. A Hail Mary pass is where a football player throws the ball as far down the field as possible, in hopes that a miracle will happen. Typically, a team will only use this play when the clock is running out and they will lose if they don't convert this attempt.

The play is named after a Catholic prayer formulation because the play is very difficult to pull off and often seems will only work through divine intervention. It is quite literally a quarterback tossing up a prayer. While Katie and I are not football players, we recognize that desperate times call for desperate measures. In our most desperate times there are no tricks to try, plans to execute, or options to choose from. In times of dire need, all we can do is pray to God, our only hope.

1. Before we dive into Jonah 1:17 and 2:1–10, spend a moment in praise, thanking God for His rescue.

Enjoy Every Word

2. Write out Jonah 1:17 and 2:1–10 below.

3. Which words or phrases in Jonah 1:17 and 2:1–10 stand out to you?

4. Record any questions you have about this passage.

Only God Almighty can bring salvation. Our merciful Creator alone can grant forgiveness of sins. Jonah learns this lesson the hard way. As he is sinking to the sea floor, he cries out to God—now knowing fully that he can do nothing to save himself.

{Salvation belongs to You, God! I am so grateful and humbled by Your choice of me. I do not deserve it. Make me a thankful, faithful servant of You and Your ways.}

IF YOU HAVE MORE TIME . . .

Foundation

Read Jonah 1:17 and 2:1–10 in a different translation.

Add Jonah 2:5–6 to your memory work. Keep reviewing verses 1–4.

OBSERVATION

[FOCUSING ON JONAH 1:17 AND 2:1–10]

> When you pass through the waters, I will be with you; and through the rivers, they shall not overwhelm you; when you walk through fire you shall not be burned, and the flame shall not consume you.
>
> —Isaiah 43:2

THE OCCASIONS THAT we've seen God work most powerfully in our lives are often unforgettable. For me (Chris), I think back to God saving my grandfather on his deathbed and the time He faithfully comforted us when our newborn daughter was in the NICU. For Katie, it was experiencing God's peace and provision through the untimely death of her twenty-nine-year-old brother. These, and more, have been deep places of pain and fear and grief. They have also been times of joy and peace and comfort.

God often allows the deep places in our lives to remind us of our need for Him. It is important for us to remember God never promises a life free from stress or hard times. God is, however, our sustainer in the midst of pain, tragedy, and hardship. Just as God allowed Jonah to sink to the depths of the sea for his good, He permits us to walk through painful places in order for His work in and around us to be completed.

1. Take a moment and reflect on your life and the occasions you've seen God work most powerfully. Thank Him for His provision during these times.

Look at the Details

2. Read Jonah 1:17 and 2:1–10, this time looking for all the actions of God. Fill in the chart with what you see.

ACTIONS OF GOD

3. Take another look at the passage. This time, determine the order in which the actions of God occurred.

ACTIONS OF GOD
(In order of occurrence.)

God's answers aren't always what we anticipated nor do they always come when we think they should arrive. Sometimes He sends unwanted and unexpected storms to provide something we weren't praying for. Yet whatever does (or doesn't) come our way, we can always expect that He hears and is working out what is best for us. God's goodness was shown in Jonah's life not only in the deliverance through the fish but also through the experience of the deeps.

{God, open my eyes to see Your deliverance all around me. Show me where You are working to bring me closer to You through deep places and stinky situations. I confess I would rather walk the easy path than the hard road, but I trust that You are in control and know what is best for me and what will bring You the most glory.}

IF YOU HAVE MORE TIME . . .

Observation

Read Jonah 1:17 and 2:1–10 again, this time paying attention to all you can learn about Jonah. Look for the following categories:

Jonah's Actions

Jonah's Realizations

Jonah's Experiences

Jonah's Response

CLARIFICATION

[FOCUSING ON JONAH 1:17 AND 2:1–10]

Every good gift and every perfect gift is from above, coming down from the Father of lights, with whom there is no variation or shadow due to change.

—James 1:17

WE HAVE A beautiful and necessary thing in our house called rest time. I (Katie) started it as a method of survival and sanity when our kids were little. It doesn't occur every day, but when we are in a good rhythm and home for the day, rest time occurs right after lunch—even as our children get older. "But Mom, I don't need to rest," and "Mom, I'm not tired," are often heard when the rest time announcement is made. Typically, it comes from the child who has shown the most need for some time alone to recharge.

I give this time to our children because I know they need it—although they certainly don't view it as a gift. Video games, movies, or playtime outside are certainly more welcomed than the dreaded household quiet time. But as their mom, who loves them more than they could ever understand (and who needs the rest herself), rest time is provided because it is what is best for all of us.

Our Father God provides for us too. We may not always view the trials in our life as a gift of love, but often the most difficult seasons of our life are exactly that—God's loving hand of correction, drawing our hearts back to His presence.

1. Ask God to show you how the difficult seasons in your life are actually for your good.

Uncover the Original Meaning

DECIDE which word you would like to study.

2. To start your Hebrew study, look for any potential key words in Jonah 1:17 and 2:1–10. As you find any repeated word or words that seem important to the passage, write them down.

DISCOVER that word as it was originally written.

3. Using your preferred tool, discover the original word for *cast* in verse 3, and write it below.

DEFINE that word.

4. Fill in the Hebrew chart for the original word you found for *cast*.

HEBREW WORD: VERSE AND VERSION:

Part of Speech:
(verb, noun, etc.)

Translation Notes:
(How else is it translated? How often is this word used?)

Strong's Concordance Number:

Definition:

Notes:

5. Choose a word from your DECIDE list, and follow the rest of the Hebrew study steps to learn more about that word.

HEBREW WORD:

VERSE AND VERSION:

Part of Speech:
(verb, noun, etc.)

Translation Notes:
(How else is it translated? How often is this word used?)

Strong's Concordance Number:

Definition:

Notes:

We may not always understand it, but God casts us into deep places, and these hard seasons are indeed a gift. It's easy to praise God through the gifts we enjoy, but it can be a struggle to praise Him when we feel as if we have nothing left. As we learn to recognize that God is in every season, we can join Jonah in a prayer of deliverance and praise.

{God, You are forever good, continually in control, and always near. Help me to see the waves and weeds as gifts You've allowed in my life for a great purpose. I'm so thankful You hear each of my prayers and see my every tear. You are my faithful deliverer.}

IF YOU HAVE MORE TIME . . .

Clarification

Follow the Hebrew study steps for additional words in Jonah 1:17 and 2:1–10. Here are a few to start with:

billows (v. 3)

pit (v. 6)

pay regard (v. 8)

UTILIZATION

[FOCUSING ON JONAH 1:17 AND 2:1–10]

Through him then let us continually offer up a sacrifice of praise to God, that is, the fruit of lips that acknowledge his name.

—Hebrews 13:15

IN THE PAST decade there has been a tremendous rise in the popularity of superhero movies. Once viewed as gimmicks, now Hollywood stars are lining up to land a spot in the next comics-based blockbuster. If you were to encounter someone with superpowers, chances are you would behave accordingly. You would not challenge someone with super-human strength to an arm-wrestling contest. You would avoid a foot race against someone with superhuman speed. You would not lie to a person with superhuman discernment.

While God is not a superhero in the comic-book sense, He does have perfect discernment. He knows our deepest thoughts, feelings, and motivations. If we come to God in prayer and aren't completely honest, He will know. There is no reason to hide as we come to God in prayer. Like Jonah, our most effective prayers are those marked by honesty and brokenness.

1. Begin with a prayer of declaration of your need for God. We don't have to wait until we're at the end of our rope before we cry out to Him.

Discover the Connections

2. Read Jonah 1:17 and 2:1–10.

3. Look up each of the following references, and take notes on what you learn.

Those who pay regard to vain idols (v. 8)

Jeremiah 14:22

Psalm 31:6–7

forsake their hope of steadfast love (v. 8)

Jeremiah 2:13

Jeremiah 17:13

Trusting in God begins with honesty—a declaration of our helplessness. Too often, we try to be the superhero ourselves, instead of seeking rescue from the only One who can bring salvation. Let's let go of our idols of pride, self-sufficiency, and capability. Instead, let's embrace our frailty and neediness. Rescue comes from God alone.

{Father, I am so thankful for Your steadfast love. When I am weary, You are strong. Though I am wayward, You are faithful. My heart is weak and wicked, yet Your salvation is complete. I praise You.}

IF YOU HAVE MORE TIME . . .

Utilization

Study Psalm 42, looking for similarities in the prayer of Jonah and the prayer of David.

Look up additional cross references for words and/or phrases in this week's passage you would like to learn more about.

SUMMATION

[FOCUSING ON JONAH 1:17 AND 2:1–10]

Bless the Lord, O my soul, and forget not all his benefits, who forgives all your iniquity, who heals all your diseases, who redeems your life from the pit, who crowns you with steadfast love and mercy, who satisfies you with good so that your youth is renewed like the eagle's.

—Psalm 103:2–5

I (KATIE) HAVE a bookshelf full of prayer journals. Decades span the dates between the first spiral-bound notebook and my current floral-bound pages. I don't journal every day, but the practice of putting my emotions to words on paper helps me connect with God. My heart has a tendency to hold onto my emotions, especially those that stem from tender, sorrowful, and broken places. So when I confess not just my sin but also my emotions, I admit my vulnerability to the only One who is able to safeguard my heart with His peace-filled presence.

Whether you enjoy the practice of journaling or primarily pray in your head to God, it is a good practice for each of us to regularly take a good look at the state of our heart and approach our Father with our fears, failures, and need for His healing. Though Jonah lacked a pen and pencil while in the fish, he spent time looking back in reflection on what he'd experienced. He was honest about his situation; He didn't sugarcoat it. The more we see the desperation of our situations, the better we will see the significance of His provision of deliverance.

Respond to God's Word

1. Take a moment to pray honestly as you begin your study. Confess your sin and your emotions. God already knows your heart. Bring it to Him.

IDENTIFY—Find the main idea of each passage.

2. Take a few moments to flip back to each day's study to review what you've learned this week. In the space below, write out Jonah 1:17 and 2:1–10 in your own words, or write out the main idea of the passage.

3. Read a commentary or study Bible to see how your observations from this week line up with the scholars.

MODIFY—Evaluate my beliefs in light of the main idea.

Journal prayerfully through the following questions, asking the Spirit of God to enlighten and convict.

4. Do I tend to continually approach God with my praise, needs, and emotions? Or do I hold onto them until I am desperate and have nowhere else to turn? Why?

5. Do I praise God for the deep places (past and/or present) in my life? Name one or two of these hard times below. As you do, write down at least one thing to praise God for in that situation.

6. When I walk through difficult seasons, do I tend to hold on to the idols of pride, self-sufficiency, and codependency, or do I cling to God's grace and faithfulness alone?

Holding on to Something or
Someone Other Than God

Clinging Desperately
to God's Grace

1   2   3   4   5   6   7   8   9   10

GLORIFY—Align my life to reflect the truth of God's Word.

7. Spend some additional time in honest prayer and worship. Write out your words below, or get on your knees in submission to our Lord. Admit your need for His rescue.

{God, I am thankful for Your Word and the many, many records of Your people clinging to You for all they need. We are frail, broken, and need You more than we can express. Make my heart's cry be for Your presence, Your plan, and Your glory to be made known to the lost around me.}

IF YOU HAVE MORE TIME . . .

Summation

Spend additional time in commentaries.

Add a title to this section in your outline in the appendix on page 174.

Grab your journal and continue the conversation with God about what He is teaching you.

Share what you are learning with a trusted friend. Ask them to pray for you as you apply what you've learned.

List all the actions and experiences of Jonah, organize them chronologically, and then sync them with the timeline you created for the actions of God on page 73.

WEEK 3: POINTS TO PONDER

[FOCUSING ON JONAH 1:17 AND 2:1–10]

God heard Jonah's prayer even though he was on a long streak of rebellious decisions.

IT IS COMFORTING to know that even when we are not at our best God's love is still available. In the same way Jonah could not outrun God's plan, he also could not outrun God's mercy. Jonah prayed in the moment of his greatest despair, and God heard him. God does not hear our prayers because we are faithful but because He is faithful.

God allowed Jonah to experience pain.

In verse 2 Jonah understands that God has played an active role in bringing about Jonah's pain. God could have stopped Jonah before he got to the sea port, on the boat, or out to sea. In His providence He allowed Jonah to experience the pain and consequences of his actions. Pain can be a gift. This is a hard teaching for most Americans who spend much of our lives attempting to avoid pain. However, sometimes the most merciful thing God can do is allow us to experience pain. For a child learning how the world works, pain is an invaluable teaching tool. It is the momentary pain of getting too close to the hot stove that prevents us from lingering and incurring permanent damage. For Jonah, the pain was real and so was the lesson. It is only when we know the reality of pain that we can enjoy salvation from it.

Jonah knew his situation was hopeless on his own but still retained hope that God could save him.

When Jonah longs to look again on God's holy temple, he is expressing his desire to be restored to fellowship with God. In fact he says this line not as a wish but as a confident assertion that he will in fact experience this reconciliation. This confidence does not come from the prophet's belief that he will find his way out of the fish or even back to shore. It is quite doubtful Jonah even knew how to swim. The assurance Jonah possesses comes from his belief that God can and will save him. That is what saving faith looks like for us too. Faith is not simply belief in our ability to earn God's love based on our moral performance; it is the steady belief that God alone saves.

God used that which looked like judgment to bring about salvation.

Most people assume the fish was God's judgment on Jonah's rebellion. Admittedly, spending three days inside a fish is a less than ideal way to cruise the Mediterranean Sea. However, it was the fish that saved Jonah from drowning. Notice as you read verses five and six that Jonah was not swallowed at the surface, but near the sea floor. With only minutes to survive, when all hope seemed lost, the fish swooped in and rescued Jonah. To many in Jesus' day, a Roman cross was a judgment reserved for the worst offenders. What looked like a symbol of judgment was really God's means of our deliverance. At the time when we were desperate, when all hope seemed lost, God sent Jesus to rescue us from the pit.

When we look to false gods we miss out on all God has to offer.

In verse 8, Jonah gives us a theological truth about idol worship. He says chasing after false gods causes us to lose our hope of steadfast love. It is a common belief that all paths lead to God. Those who advocate this position see all the world religions as basically the same with only different terminology or methods to accomplish the same means. Jonah rejects this view and says those who worship something other than the one true God will not experience God's love at all. This is not just true of those who worship little statues; an idol is anything we value more than God. Our idols can be good things like relationships, work, children, or health. If we place more value on these things than we place on worshipping the one, true God, we are guilty of idol worship.

God is honored by our repentance.

The lesson God was teaching Jonah seems to be learned in verse 9 when Jonah vows to make right the situation with Nineveh. In light of the consequence of running from God, Jonah has a change of heart, leading to a change in action. This is what repentance looks like. On one hand, repentance is not simply changing sinful actions. God desires more than behavior modification. On the other, true repentance requires a turn from the actual sin. Additionally, repentance is not simply feeling badly about our sin. Repentance means we no longer see the sin as preferable. Instead, we desire what God desires.

WEEK 3: CHEAT SHEET

Day 2: Observation

2. Read Jonah 1:17 and 2:1–10, this time looking for all the actions of God. Fill in the chart with what you see.

ACTIONS OF GOD

Appointed a fish to swallow up Jonah (v. 17)
Answered Jonah's call out of distress (v. 2)
Heard Jonah's cry from the belly of Sheol (v. 2)
Cast Jonah into the deep/heart of the seas (v. 3)
Brought Jonah's life up from the pit (v. 6)
Spoke to the fish, to vomit Jonah onto dry land (v. 10)

3. Take another look at the passage. This time, determine the order in which the actions of God occurred.

ACTIONS OF GOD
(In order of occurrence.)

1. Cast Jonah into the deep/heart of the seas (v. 3)

2. Heard Jonah's cry from the belly of Sheol (v. 2)

3. Answered Jonah's call out of distress (v. 2)
Brought Jonah's life up from the pit (v. 6)
Appointed a fish to swallow up Jonah (v. 17)

4. Spoke to the fish, to vomit Jonah onto dry land (v. 10)

Day 3: Clarification

4. Fill in the Hebrew chart for the original word you found for *cast*.

HEBREW WORD:
slk or shalak

VERSE AND VERSION:
Jonah 2:3 ESV

Part of Speech:
(verb, noun, etc.)

verb

Translation Notes:
(How else is it translated? How often is this word used?)

used 125 times in the Old Testament, 61 of those translate to "cast"

Strong's Concordance Number:
H7993

Definition:
to throw; to eject, dispose of, remove, scatter

Notes:

the uses of this action vary greatly [James Swanson, Dictionary of Biblical Languages with Semantic Domains: Hebrew (Old Testament). Oak Harbor: Logos Research Systems, Inc., 1997.]

WEEK 4

I would go into the deeps a hundred times to cheer a down-cast spirit: it is good for me to have been afflicted that I might know how to speak a word in season to one that is weary.
—CHARLES SPURGEON, *THE SOUL-WINNER*

Without a heart transformed by the grace of Christ, we just continue to manage external and internal darkness.
—MATT CHANDLER, *THE EXPLICIT GOSPEL*

THE TWENTIETH CENTURY was the setting for the largest military conflict of all time, World War II. Never before had the world seen one war affect nearly every corner of the globe. The context of war presents an opportunity for individuals to rise to the occasion and become enshrined as legendary heroes. For the Unites States names like MacArthur, Patton, and Eisenhower evoke patriotism. Across the pond, in the United Kingdom, the name that towers over all others is Churchill. In fact, it would be difficult to accurately tell the story of WWII without understanding the importance of Britain's most well known prime minister.

Winston Churchill stood in opposition to Hitler and the brutal Nazi regime at a time when many European leaders could not. It may surprise you to find out, however, that Churchill was an unlikely candidate to lead the UK. Although Churchill held several positions of prominence before and during the First World War, in the years leading up to WWII he found himself out of politics altogether. Churchill was somewhat of a disgraced figure following WWI. He was the major architect of the failed Allied attack plan at the Battle of Gallipoli, and Churchill took the brunt of the blame. He was demoted, and he eventually resigned.

When Britain was looking for leadership heading into another global conflict, one of the last names they expected to rise to prominence was Winston Churchill's. It was only after the naive (and failed) attempts at diplomacy from then Prime Minister Neville Chamberlain that Churchill again came to power. Chamberlain believed the evils of the Nazi's could be handled diplomatically. What Chamberlain saw as diplomacy, Hitler saw as weakness and opportunity. Once the Germans began their assault on the European continent, it was clear the UK needed a strong leader who understood the depths of Nazi depravity.

Winston Churchill's leadership was a major factor in the Allied powers winning WWII. Churchill's rise to power was not simply a tale of one man rising to the occasion but also a tale of redemption—a man making the most of his second chance.

This week we will see all the principle players in the Book of Jonah receive a second chance. Jonah gets a second chance when God recommissions him to the assignment to go to Nineveh. The people of Nineveh get a second chance because they heed Jonah's warning and repent of their wickedness.

God's love and mercy are on full display as He gives second chances not only to a pagan city but also a faithless prophet.

FOUNDATION

[FOCUSING ON JONAH 3]

For their sake he remembered his covenant, and relented according to the abundance of his steadfast love.

—Psalm 106:45

WHEN WE MOVED into our current house there was no washer and dryer. We promptly went to the hardware store and bought a set that seemed like a good purchase. It was a brand that came highly respected. It was not the cheapest set they offered, but it was not an expensive pair, either.

About two years ago we started experiencing problems with the washing machine. It was under warranty, but it took the repairman a month to come out, then another month to get the parts in to fix it. A few months later the washing machine broke down yet again. And again, it took the repairman about a month to come out, and another few weeks to get the part. This time, however, the part did not fix the problem, and he declared it a total loss. The warranty covered a complete replacement for the unit.

So we found ourselves shopping for another washing machine at the hardware store. The salesman assured us the problem was not with the brand; we must have had a lemon. We decided to give the brand another shot. We have been happy with the purchase until about a month ago when we got a notice in the mail that the machine has been recalled and will need to be replaced.

If you were us, would you give the brand another shot, or is that company essentially dead to you? Many of us are willing to give a second chance but eventually will draw the line and say, "No more." Likewise, we are tempted to view God as having limits to His mercy. We think He might give up on us if we blow our second chance. However, as we will see this week, God is a God of second chances (and third and fourth chances too). Both Jonah and the Ninevites experience the patience of our God.

1. Before we dive into Jonah 3, spend a moment in prayer. Ask God to open your eyes to the glory of His patient mercy.

Enjoy Every Word

2. Write out Jonah 3 below.

3. Which words or phrases in Jonah 3 stand out to you?

4. Write out any questions you have about this passage.

The Bible points again and again to the patient heart of God. Yes, He is holy. Yes, He is judge. But He is also merciful and desires for all to come to repentance. No matter how far we've drifted or how long we've strayed, He is always willing, able, and ready to forgive.

> {God, I am so grateful for Your mercy. Thank You for saving me from my sin. I praise You for Your grace shown toward me and the fact that Your grip on me has more to do with Your faithful character than mine. Help me to make the most of my second chances. May You be glorified through Your work in me.}

IF YOU HAVE MORE TIME . . .

Foundation

Read Jonah 3 in a different translation.

Add Jonah 2:7–8 to your memory work.

OBSERVATION

[FOCUSING ON JONAH 3]

"Rend your hearts and not your garments." Return to the LORD your God, for he is gracious and merciful, slow to anger, and abounding in steadfast love; and he relents over disaster.

—Joel 2:13

KATIE AND I met in Jacksonville, Florida, and as newlyweds, we lived near the Arlington Expressway. This road starts out as a divided highway and turns into a limited access road (think interstate highway). At the point where this change happens, there is a residential side street, which is your last chance to get of the expressway before it turns into the interstate-style road.

I had exited the expressway onto this side street many times but never attempted to merge back onto the expressway when coming back the other way. One day I attempted to do just that, but instead of merging onto the eastbound lane, I found myself in the westbound lane . . . heading east. Now facing oncoming traffic—and trying to stay off the six o'clock news—I needed to get off that street, and fast! Desperately, I looked for a place to turn around to no avail. Just before the next wave of traffic approached, I decided to hop a curb and drive through a median (and perhaps someone's yard) until I got to a road where I could head the right direction.

There was a difference between wanting to turn around and actually turning around. Until I actually made the turn I was headed toward trouble. Once my direction was changed, the crisis was averted. This is the biblical picture of repentance—to change direction and turn away from the danger our sin leads us into. It's not enough to merely recognize we are headed the wrong way; repentance is actually making the turn.

1. Ask the Holy Spirit to grant you the grace needed for true repentance. Open your heart to His gentle conviction. Commit to turn and walk away from the sin He addresses.

Look at the Details

2. Start with Jonah 3:2–3, paying attention to what is true about the city of Nineveh. Note all you learn about the city of Nineveh in the following chart. Then read Jonah 1:2 and add to your list. Look ahead to Jonah 4:11 and add anything you learn about the city of Nineveh to your chart.

TRUTHS ABOUT NINEVEH

3. Read Jonah 3, and focus on the actions of the king and the people of Nineveh.

ACTIONS OF THE PEOPLE	ACTIONS OF THE KING

Nineveh's response is a true picture of repentance. It was a screeching halt from their wicked ways. It was not only an emotional response, nor was it a simple recognition that their position was sinful. Nineveh's newfound belief in God resulted in swift and striking action. And God relented. Though God is indeed holy and must punish sin, He is also compassionate and responds with mercy to truly repentant hearts.

{God, may I never take Your mercy for granted! I confess my often-lackadaisical approach to the reality of my sin. Grant me the same fervor to abandon my wicked ways as the nation of Nineveh displayed. I'm so thankful for Your patient and merciful character.}

IF YOU HAVE MORE TIME . . .

Observation

Note and record the actions of Jonah.

Note and record the actions of God.

CLARIFICATION

[FOCUSING ON JONAH 3]

For godly grief produces a repentance that leads to salvation without regret, whereas worldly grief produces death.

—2 Corinthians 7:10

WE ARE EASILY offended as a culture. It seems everyday some public figure or company is vilified in the court of public opinion for some thoughtless word or unpopular position. The expected response is for the offender to trot out behind a podium and deliver an apology that was clearly written by a team of public relations professionals and lawyers.

You may have also experienced these types of half-hearted apologies from a friend or family member. The worst apologies are the ones that include the clause, "I apologize if I have offended you . . ." Really what that person is saying is, "I'm only sorry if someone is offended." Everyone sees this weak apology for what it is—inauthentic. Authentic apologies require genuine sorrow, not a sadness that someone was offended, but remorse over the wrong that was committed.

1. Ask the Spirit to continue His work in your heart today as you study.

Uncover the Original Meaning

DECIDE which word you would like to study.

2. To start your Hebrew study, look for any potential key words in Jonah 3. As you find any repeated word or words that seem important to the passage, write them down.

DISCOVER that word as it was originally written.

3. Using your preferred tool, discover the original word for *sackcloth* used in verses 5, 6, and 8, and write it below.

DEFINE that word.

4. Fill in the Hebrew chart for the original word you found for *sackcloth*.

HEBREW WORD: VERSE AND VERSION:

Part of Speech: *(verb, noun, etc.)*	Translation Notes: *(How else is it translated? How often is this word used?)*
Strong's Concordance Number:	Definition:

Notes:

5. Choose a word from your DECIDE list, and follow the rest of the Hebrew study steps to learn more about that word.

HEBREW WORD:

VERSE AND VERSION:

Part of Speech:
(verb, noun, etc.)

Translation Notes:
(How else is it translated? How often is this word used?)

Strong's Concordance Number:

Definition:

Notes:

Another key component of repentance is true sorrow and a brokenhearted posture over our sin. This is what we see the Ninevites doing as they put on sackcloth and ashes. Used often as a sign of mourning, taking on sackcloth (which was extremely uncomfortable) and ashes (a sign that we are but dust) was a common action for this culture to demonstrate their grief and humility over a situation. In this case, for the Ninevites, it was their grief over their wickedness and their humility before the Lord.

{Lord, my sin is great, but I'm thankful Your mercy is greater. I praise You for rescuing me and for relenting over the punishment I deserve. Jesus, thank You for taking on that wrath and for providing new life for me to walk in for eternity.}

IF YOU HAVE MORE TIME . . .

Clarification

Follow the Hebrew study steps to look up the following words (and look up any other words you want to know more about) from Jonah 3:

message (v. 2)

overthrown (v. 4)

issued (v. 7)

UTILIZATION

[FOCUSING ON JONAH 3]

> Their heart was not steadfast toward him; they were not faithful to his covenant. Yet he, being compassionate, atoned for their iniquity and did not destroy them; he restrained his anger often and did not stir up all his wrath.
>
> —Psalm 78:37–38

AS PARENTS, WE are tasked with the discipline of our children. Discipline is difficult and there are many pitfalls for parents. On one hand you don't want to be a pushover, and on the other you don't want to be unnecessarily punitive. Add to this balancing act the realization that everyone else has an opinion on how you discipline your kids and usually aren't afraid to let you know it.

In our passage this week, we see our perfect Father responding in love without wavering in truth. In Nineveh, God is not seen as a pushover. They understood the holiness, power, and wrath of God. If they did not change course, they would be destroyed. He was not seen as overly harsh but justly angry over their sin. Yet God does not punish the Ninevites after they repent. He relents from His anger and accepts their penitent hearts. The end goal of God's discipline was not the punishment, or else He would have struck them down regardless of their response. The intention of correction was an admission and contrition over their sin.

1. Begin by thanking God for His great mercy.

Discover the Connections

2. Read Jonah 3 to start your study.

3. Look up each of the following references, and take notes on what you learn.

   arose from his throne, removed his robe, covered himself with sackcloth (v. 6)

   Job 1:20

   turn from his evil way (v. 8)

   Romans 2:4

   2 Peter 3:9

turn from his fierce anger (v. 9)

Psalm 78:38–39

Psalm 85:2–3

Romans 1:18

God's response to the truly repentant is always mercy. The Bible has a wonderful message of hope for those who repent: God relents from the punishment stored up for our sin when we forsake it and turn to Him. However, there is no good news in Scripture for those who do not repent. As a just and righteous judge, God takes sin seriously and will not lower the bar for sinners. Fortunately, He is also a loving Father who Has provided a way—through Christ—for those who repent and trust in His ways.

{God, I am humbled by Your provision of Your Son so that I might receive Your mercy. I praise You for Your steadfast love for me and patience with me. Though I am fractured and forgetful, You are faithful. Though I fail and founder, You forgive. I'm so thankful.}

IF YOU HAVE MORE TIME . . .

Utilization

Look up additional instances of mourning through sackcloth and ashes:

Genesis 37:29–34

2 Samuel 3:31–32

Follow additional cross references for words and/or phrases in this week's passage you would like to learn more about.

SUMMATION

[FOCUSING ON JONAH 3]

But I received mercy for this reason, that in me, as the foremost, Jesus Christ might display his perfect patience as an example to those who were to believe in him for eternal life.

—1 Timothy 1:16

WHO IS THE hardest person in your life to love? Maybe it is that coworker who is always making your life difficult. It could be that family member you dread seeing at family gatherings. Or perhaps it is a neighbor who makes living on your street uncomfortable. It's easy to despise the difficult people in our lives and challenging to show them the love and mercy of God.

Jonah struggled to bring the message of mercy to the Ninevites. Thus, the running from God. Patiently, God provided Jonah with a second chance, and Jonah took it. He was recommissioned to bring God's goodness to the wicked nation of Nineveh.

Though Jonah did not completely learn the lesson of showing mercy to those who don't deserve it (as we will see next week), he still moved toward obedience, and God used Him to bring a nation to its knees in worship of the one true God. This reluctant prophet was guilty of racism, nationalistic pride, abandonment, blatant rebellion, hypocrisy, and immaturity. Yet God used Him to bring salvation to thousands of souls. In fact, God has a tendency to use the weak and weary, the insignificant and incompetent, and the unlikely and unconventional to do His work. In doing so, instead of man being lifted up, God gets the glory.

Respond to God's Word

1. Pray to the Spirit of God, once again offering up your heart for inspection.

IDENTIFY—Find the main idea of each passage.

2. Take a few moments to flip back to each day's study to review what you've learned this week. Write out Jonah 3 in your own words, or write out the main idea of Jonah 3.

3. Read a commentary or study Bible to see how your observations from this week line up with the scholars.

MODIFY—Evaluate my beliefs in light of the main idea.

Journal prayerfully through the following questions, asking the Spirit of God to enlighten and convict.

4. When given a second chance to obey God's commands, do I tend to take it or do I wallow in the paralysis of failure?

5. How do I typically respond to the chastening of God?

*Ignore Conviction
and Try to Avoid
His Presence*

*Immediately and
Specifically Confess My
Sin and Turn Away from It*

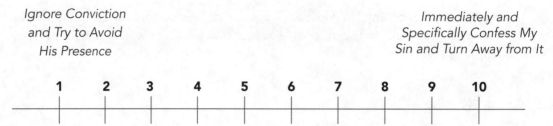

6. Are there any people (or groups of people) that I refuse to have compassion for? If so, why do I struggle to show mercy toward them?

GLORIFY—Align my life to reflect the truth of God's Word.

7. Write out at least one sin God is convicting you of. This could be something new He's brought to the surface this week or something you've struggled with for a long time.

8. Spend some time in prayer over this area of your life. If you are not yet sorrowful over this sin, ask God to break your heart over your transgression. Confess the specifics; agree with God that it is wrong and an offense toward Him. State your desire to return to His ways. Ask for the grace to walk away from your sin and toward the presence of God. Thank Him for His mercy.

{Oh, how I need You, God! I need Your conviction. I need Your mercy. I need Your grace. I need Your presence and the power and freedom You provide over my sin. Help me, Lord. Make me more and more like Your precious and holy Son.}

IF YOU HAVE MORE TIME . . .

Summation

Spend additional time in commentaries.

Add a title to this section in your outline in the appendix on page 174.

Grab your journal and continue the conversation with God about what He is teaching you.

Share what you are learning with a trusted friend. Ask them to pray for you as you apply what you've learned.

List all the actions and experiences of Jonah, organize them chronologically, and then sync them with the timeline you created for the actions of God on page 95.

WEEK 4: POINTS TO PONDER

[FOCUSING ON JONAH 3]

God is a God of second chances.

IN CHAPTER THREE, both Jonah and the people of Nineveh come to learn that God is a God of second chances. In verse 1, Jonah receives the word from God a second time. We can only image what it was like for Jonah to hear God's voice again. Like water on a dry riverbed the message permeates the cracks and crevices of Jonah's heart until he is overflowing with the sense of restoration that only comes from being in a right relationship with God. Similarly, the people of Nineveh receive a second chance from God. Jonah's message as he walks the streets is a warning of impending destruction. Interestingly, Jonah never tells Nineveh that their repentance will result in a stay of God's hand. In verse 4, Jonah only states they will experience disaster in forty days. Yet in verse 10 God indeed spares Nineveh from the promised destruction. The people of this city receive a second chance from God. It is encouraging to note that God gives second chances to faithless prophets and idol worshipping pagans—He also gives second chances to you and me.

Complete obedience is required, even when incomplete information is given.

At the beginning of the chapter God commands Jonah to go to Nineveh before He gave him the message he was to speak. Jonah had to demonstrate trust and obedience to God by setting out before he had all the details. How many of us are willing to make life-changing decisions to go to dangerous places without knowing every facet of the plan? God often commands believers to set out with incomplete information. The Psalmist promises God's Word is a lamp unto our feet and a light unto our path (Psalm 119:105). The thing about Bronze Age lamps on a dark path is they only give off enough light to illuminate a few steps ahead. God doesn't promise to give us all of the details, nor does obedience to His will require us to know them. We may not always know the particulars of God's plan, but we are expected to follow it nonetheless.

God loves cities.

Nineveh was a city of 120,000 people (Jonah 4:11). Each one of these inhabitants was a human created in the image of God. The Lord knows every inhabitant of every city that has ever existed. As a person accustomed to small town life, I (Chris) sometimes view cities as big, scary places where evil and secularism tend to congregate. In Jonah, God demonstrates His concern for cities in an undeniable way. This is not an exception in the Bible; it seems to be more the rule. When Paul goes on his missionary journeys in Acts he seeks out urban areas. Most of the New Testament is letters written to churches in cities. God loved the cities of the Ancient Near East in Jonah's time, and He loves cities today.

Effective ministry requires the favor of God.

Jonah's ministry was effective because God blessed it, not because of Jonah's cleverness or creativity. Remember, Jonah was no model minister. He was reluctant to go to these people, and later we will see his heart never truly loved them. Additionally, Jonah's message was short and offensive. The prophet utters a few words of warning. Other than that we have no record of his ministry in that city. However, in terms of response, Jonah is one of the most effective ministers in the Bible. We cannot draw any other conclusion from Jonah's ministry than his effectiveness had more to do with God than with Jonah. In the same way, success in our personal ministry to others does not depend on our ability, attractiveness, or eloquence. The greatest factor in the success of our personal ministry is the favor of God. Instead of asking God to make you better at ministering to people, ask Him to place His favor upon you.

There is no good news for those who don't repent.

This message is true in the Book of Jonah and in the rest of the Bible as well. Had Nineveh failed to heed the warning there is no doubt they would have been overthrown. The death toll would have been astronomical. The level of human suffering would have been excruciating. Fortunately, this city repents and avoids such disaster. In the same way, the Bible is a great message of hope for sinners. The gospel means good news. The goods news is that Jesus Christ is the answer to our sin problem and faith in Him results in forgiveness of sin and eternal life. In order to experience the benefits of salvation the New Testament repeatedly commands us to repent and believe. However, the gospel contains no good news for people who fail to repent. God is a God of mercy and grace whose love is unconditionally applied to believers because of Christ. But make no mistake, God's mercy does not negate His justice—He will punish sin. Those who reject Christ's offer of salvation are left to pay for their sin, which will take an eternity.

WEEK 4: CHEAT SHEET

Day 2: Observation

2. Start with Jonah 3:2–3, paying attention to what is true about the city of Nineveh. Note all you learn about the city of Nineveh in the following chart. Then read Jonah 1:2 and add to your list. Look ahead to Jonah 4:11 and add anything you learn about the city of Nineveh to your chart.

TRUTHS ABOUT NINEVEH

Great city (3:2)
Exceedingly great city (3:3)
Three days' journey in breadth (3:3)

Great city (1:2)
Their evil had come up before God (1:2)

Great city (4:11)
More than 120,000 persons (4:11)
The people "do not know their right hand from their left" (4:11)
Much cattle (4:11)

3. Read Jonah 3, and focus on the actions of the king and the people of Nineveh.

ACTIONS OF THE PEOPLE

Believed God (v. 5)
Called for a fast (v. 5)
Put on sackcloth (v. 5)

ACTIONS OF THE KING

Covered himself with sackcloth (v. 6)
Sat in ashes (v. 6)
Issued a proclamation for all to: (v. 7–8)
fast; take on sackcloth; "call out mightily to God"; turn from evil ways; turn from violence

Day 3: Clarification

4. Fill in the Hebrew chart for the original word you found for *sackcloth*.

HEBREW WORD:
saq

VERSE AND VERSION:
Jonah 3:5, 6, 8 ESV

Part of Speech:
(verb, noun, etc.)

noun

Translation Notes:
(How else is it translated? How often is this word used?)

used 48 times, 42 of those are "sackcloth"

Strong's Concordance Number:

H8242

Definition:

sack, blanket

Notes:

"the dress of mourners" [Wilhelm Gesenius and Samuel Prideaux Tregelles. Gesenius' Hebrew and Chaldee Lexicon to the Old Testament Scriptures. Bellingham, WA: Logos Bible Software, 2003), 794]; worn in mourning or humiliation. [James Strong, Enhanced Strong's Lexicon. Woodside Bible Fellowship, 1995]

WEEK 5

FOCUSING ON JONAH 4

Every saved person this side of heaven owes the gospel to every lost person this side of hell.
—DAVID PLATT, *RADICAL*

God is pursuing with omnipotent passion a worldwide purpose of gathering joyful worshipers for Himself from every tribe and tongue and people and nation. He has an inexhaustible enthusiasm for the supremacy of His name among the nations.
—JOHN PIPER, *LET THE NATIONS BE GLAD!*

HAVE YOU EVER wondered why most grocery stores have a similar layout? It doesn't matter if you go to Walmart or Whole Foods. Certain patterns emerge in nearly every store. Fresh produce will be close to the front door, items like meat, seafood, milk, and eggs will line the outer edges, while dry goods and frozen items will fill the aisles in the middle. Grocery store companies have spent years perfecting this layout. Today's supermarkets are set up with almost surgical precision to elicit the most money from your pocket.

One tactic these stores employ to increase profitability is placing all of the most attractive cereal brands at eye-level with children. Doesn't it seem as though every time you see a child throwing a fit in the grocery store it is in the middle of the cereal aisle? This is no coincidence; this is very much by design. These companies know it is highly embarrassing for parents to be the one whose child is convulsing on the floor. To provide an easily accessible exit nearest the cereal aisle might entice some parents to run. By placing the cereal in the middle of the store it is easier to buy the box of Fruity Wheels than to run the risk of looking like a kidnapper at the local Shop-N-Save.

As horrific as it is to think of your child being the petulant one writhing on a supermarket floor, this is exactly what we see Jonah doing in chapter 4. Jonah is so displeased with

God's mercy he throws an absolute fit. Jonah would rather die than live in a world where Assyrians receive God's mercy. Jonah preposterously values the life of a plant more than any of the Ninevites he saw along his journey. We are even told the only reason Jonah sticks around Nineveh is to watch God destroy it.

The book ends with Jonah's heart still callous toward the people of Nineveh and the will of God. Jonah is perhaps the most successful prophet in the Old Testament while at the same time being one of the least worthy of emulation. This book is a complex journey through the inner workings of a hard-hearted man. The fact that God never destroys Jonah is encouraging to people like us who often find ourselves callous to the lost and hesitant to do the will of God.

As you study this week, pray that God will give you the ability to see clearly the inner workings of your own heart.

WEEK 5 | DAY 1

FOUNDATION

[FOCUSING ON JONAH 4]

It is the LORD who goes before you. He will be with you; he will not leave you or forsake you. Do not fear or be dismayed.

—Deuteronomy 31:8

WITHOUT SPEED LIMITS I (Chris) would drive much faster that I do. I love driving, and I hate going slow. On the other hand, I am also a rule follower at heart and have little desire to catch the attention of the police. Additionally, I am cheap, and I don't want to spend money on speeding tickets. Speed limits, the police who enforce them, and the penalties they can dole out each act as correctives for my right foot.

In the same way that local and state governments establish these measures to correct overzealous drivers, God appoints corrective influences in our lives. In our passage this week we see God appoints a plant, a worm, and the wind to correct the waywardness in Jonah's heart.

1. Before we dive into Jonah 4, spend a moment in prayer. Ask God to open your eyes to the attitudes of Jonah as an evaluator for your own.

Enjoy Every Word

2. Write out Jonah 4.

3. Which words or phrases in Jonah 4 stand out to you?

4. Record any questions you have about this passage.

Our Father in Heaven knows us better than we know ourselves. He knows our struggles, our sin, and the strain they will bring to our lives. God always wants what is best for us. His plan is good. His ways are right. And when we stray, He lovingly sends interventions as corrective influences over our lives. He does not send these corrections out of hate but out of love. God loves us too much to leave us in our spiritual immaturity.

{God, I thank You for Your loving hand in my life. It is not always easy to experience Your correction, but I trust that Your ways are best. I do want to walk according to Your will. Thank You for the guardrails you appoint that keep me on track.}

IF YOU HAVE MORE TIME . . .

Foundation

Read Jonah 4 in a different translation.
Add Jonah 2:9 to your memory work.

OBSERVATION

[FOCUSING ON JONAH 4]

My brothers, show no partiality as you hold the faith in our Lord Jesus Christ, the Lord of glory.

—James 2:1

EVERY FOUR YEARS national patriotism spikes as the Summer Olympics come around. From the pageantry of the opening ceremony to the victorious athletes on the podium, each country celebrates the athletic achievement with support and national pride.

There is nothing wrong with patriotism or gratefulness for the blessings of being a citizen of the United States. However, we must always guard against finding our identity in our nationality. As Christians we are not primarily citizens of any earthly nation but of the kingdom of the Living God. As citizens of that kingdom we have brothers and sisters all around the world and many more who will be our family members. We must never let our national pride take priority over our desire to see others come into the kingdom.

1. Ask God to reveal any places of national or racial pride that hinders your ability to willingly share the gospel with all people.

Look at the Details

2. Start by reading Jonah 4:1–4. Pay special attention to Jonah and the attitudes and emotions he conveyed about God's decision to show mercy to the nation of Nineveh.

ATTITUDES AND EMOTIONS OF JONAH IN 4:1–4

3. Now focus on Jonah 4:5–9, looking at Jonah's attitudes and emotions toward God's appointment of the plant and the worm.

ATTITUDES AND EMOTIONS OF JONAH IN 4:5–9

Jonah was blinded by borders and ethnicity and failed to recognize that God's love is not confined to any one race of people or area on the map. Jonah chose pride over pity—failing to see that we all need mercy—and was more disturbed over the fate of the plant than the thousands of souls in need of rescue.

{God, I confess I hold prejudices toward people not like me. I have walked in pride of all I am (and am not) and have failed to see that all I have is a gift from You. You appointed the time and place of my birth, and every talent and ability, paycheck, and opportunity is an undeserved gift of grace from You.}

IF YOU HAVE MORE TIME . . .

Observation

Note the characteristics of God declared by Jonah in 4:2.

Note the actions of God in this passage and what that teaches you about the character of God.

CLARIFICATION

[FOCUSING ON JONAH 4]

I have great sorrow and unceasing anguish in my heart. For I could wish that I myself were accursed and cut off from Christ for the sake of my brothers.

—Romans 9:2–3

THROUGH THE TECHNOLOGICAL advances over the last century, the coverage of global news and events becomes more available every year. And with the dawn of social media, the dissemination of realities found on each continent is quicker and less filtered than ever. News that used to take weeks or days to make it around the world can now be revealed—even viewed by anyone with an Internet connection—through live streaming. One of the realities that has been unveiled in greater measure is the persecution of Christians throughout the world.

Oppressors believe punitive actions will stop the spread of Christianity. Yet, history has proven that the countries with the most persecution of Christians are also the places where the church is thriving and spreading like wildfire. Many think persecution is a work of the evil one, yet that oppression only leads to more souls coming to Christ. Jesus promised to build His church and that the gates of hell will not prevail against it. A frontal attack will not work against the bride of Christ.

Satan knows that more effective than making Christianity uncomfortable is making it very comfortable. He knows that if Christians spend more time thinking about their comfort than the spiritual condition of others, he can blunt our influence in the world. Churches split over issues that don't matter. Christians walk away from the church because their selfish desires are not met. Leaders compromise their integrity and vision to keep the peace. Discomfort doesn't stop the gospel from advancing. Comfort does.

1. Ask God to open your eyes to the places in your life that have become too comfortable. Pray for the resolve and strength to lay aside that which hinders you from living a life of sacrifice for the sake of the gospel.

Uncover the Original Meaning

DECIDE which word you would like to study.

2. To start your Hebrew study, look for any potential key words in Jonah 4. As you find any repeated word or words that seem important to the passage, write them down.

DISCOVER that word as it was originally written.

3. Using your preferred tool, discover the original word for *pity* in verses 10 and 11.

DEFINE that word.

4. Fill in the Hebrew chart for the original word you found for *pity*.

HEBREW WORD: VERSE AND VERSION:

Part of Speech:
(verb, noun, etc.)

Translation Notes:
(How else is it translated? How often is this word used?)

Strong's Concordance Number:

Definition:

Notes:

5. Choose a word from your DECIDE list, and follow the rest of the Hebrew study steps to learn more about that word.

HEBREW WORD: VERSE AND VERSION:

Part of Speech: .
(verb, noun, etc.)

Translation Notes:
(How else is it translated? How often is this word used?)

Strong's Concordance Number: Definition:

Notes:

As he awaits the destruction of Nineveh, Jonah finds comfort under the shade of a plant. When God takes that plant away, Jonah throws a hissy fit for the ages, revealing he cares more about the destiny of the weed than the souls of more than 120,000 people. Jonah was disturbed by the disruption of his comfort—willing to die to show his displeasure—yet not at all moved by compassion for the lost souls of Nineveh.

{May I not be like Jonah! Help me, Lord. Change my heart. Make it beat as Yours does, wishing that all would come to repentance. Grant me the same sorrow Paul showed over the lost. Move me to action for the sake of the lost.}

IF YOU HAVE MORE TIME . . .

Clarification

Follow the Hebrew study steps to look up the following words (and look up any other words you want to know more about) from Jonah 4.

displeased (v. 1)

angry (vv. 1, 4, 9)

love (v. 2)

appointed (vv. 6, 7, 8)

UTILIZATION

[FOCUSING ON JONAH 4]

> God looks down from heaven on the children of man to see
> if there are any who understand, who seek after God. They
> have all fallen away; together they have become corrupt;
> there is none who does good, not even one.
>
> —Psalm 53:2–3

NOT ALL INSULTS are received with the same amount of pain. We place more weight on some hurts than others. For instance, you may be reduced to tears if your best friend told you, "I don't like you anymore." However, if you heard the same statement from a child you just sent to timeout, you may laugh. Like many things in life, meaning depends on the source.

Oftentimes Christians respond to insults from the lost with venom, hostility, and hatred. This makes as much sense as sticking our tongue out at the kid on her way to time out who proclaims she no longer likes us. Rather than taking offense at unbelievers and responding with hate, Christians are called to absorb these slights and respond with love.

At the end of this book God taught Jonah that the lost in Nineveh "don't know their right hand from their left" (v. 11). God's point to the faithless prophet is that the lostness of Nineveh should not surprise Jonah. They don't know any other way. He should have expected them to act like lost people because they were lost people.

1. Ask God to give you His eyes for the lost around you. Confess your unrealistic expectations of those who do not know Him. Ask God for a heart filled with compassion for those who are without Christ.

Discover the Connections

2. Start your study time today by reading Jonah 4.

3. Look up each of the following references, and take notes on what you learn.

you are a gracious God . . . relenting from disaster (v. 2)

Joel 2:12–14

Psalm 86:5

1 Timothy 2:3–4

2 Peter 3:9

When we learn to view every soul through the lens of God's merciful patience, it is much harder to remain angry with them. Each of us, without Christ, are a massive mess. How much more are those who live without the compass and hope that life with Christ provides?

{God, I confess my arrogance and pride toward those who are with-out Christ. I am all-too-often forgetful of the urgent need nonbelievers have for Your mercy. Make me a vessel of Your grace.}

IF YOU HAVE MORE TIME . . .

Clarification

There are many passages in Job we could look at, but notice the parallels in Job's response to God and Jonah's questioning of God's ways.

for it is better for me to die than to live (v. 3)

Job 3:11–26

Do you do well to be angry? (v. 4)

Job 40:1–8

Look up additional cross references for words and/or phrases in this week's passage that you would like to learn more about.

SUMMATION

[FOCUSING ON JONAH 4]

Do nothing from selfish ambition or conceit, but in humility count others more significant than yourselves.

—Philippians 2:3

MY (CHRIS'S) GRANDFATHER was a career fireman, ultimately rising to the rank of fire chief in my hometown. Perhaps this is why I have always admired first responders. Whether it is a fireman, paramedic, or police officer we can all think of times when we relied on these men and women to serve and protect. One of the common traits of these often-underappreciated civil servants is bravery. These heroes run to the danger when many others would run away.

The Bible gives us portraits of many different heroes. The stories of their faith provide us with attitudes and actions to adopt. However, we also see many stories of individuals who were less than heroic. Theirs are stories we can learn from as well. They give us examples to avoid. Though the Book of Jonah is not filled with commands for us to fulfill, there is much we can apply to our everyday living.

Jonah ran the opposite way hoping to save his own hide. He chose safety over submission to God's good plan. Even after he turned around and begrudgingly obeyed, he chose pride over pity and comfort over compassion. Though the story of Jonah doesn't give us much by way of our to-do list, there is ample opportunity for us to take a good look in the mirror to see if we look more like Jonah than we care to admit.

Whereas Jonah would do anything to escape bringing a message of mercy to the lost, Jesus did whatever it took.

Respond to God's Word

1. Spend a few moments thanking God for His rescue of your soul. Express your gratitude for His continued working in you.

IDENTIFY—Find the main idea of each passage.

2. Take a few moments to flip back to each day's study to review what you've learned this week. In the space below, write out Jonah 4 in your own words, or write out the main idea of Jonah 4.

3. Read a commentary or study Bible to see how your observations from this week line up with the scholars.

MODIFY—Evaluate my beliefs in light of the main idea.

As we wrap up our study of Jonah, prayerfully rank yourself and then journal your reactions to each question.

4. When prompted by the Spirit of God to move forward in obedience in uncertain situations, how do I tend to react?

Safety over
Submission

Immediately Following
Wherever He Leads

```
    1     2     3     4     5     6     7     8     9     10
    |     |     |     |     |     |     |     |     |     |
----+-----+-----+-----+-----+-----+-----+-----+-----+-----+----
    |     |     |     |     |     |     |     |     |     |
```

5. When interacting with people who have offended, harmed, and/or scared me or my loved ones, what do I tend to show in my interactions with them?

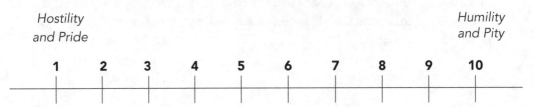

Hostility and Pride   *Humility and Pity*

1   2   3   4   5   6   7   8   9   10

6. What does the way I spend my time, money, energy, and talents communicate?

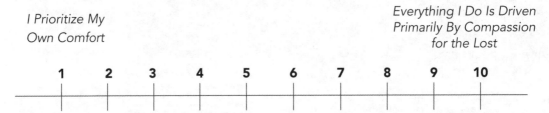

I Prioritize My Own Comfort   *Everything I Do Is Driven Primarily By Compassion for the Lost*

1   2   3   4   5   6   7   8   9   10

GLORIFY—Align my life to reflect the truth of God's Word.

7. Ask God to bring change in your ability to walk forward in obedience. Declare your desire to choose submission over safety.

8. Confess any national, cultural, or racial pride you've held on to. Ask God to change your heart in this area. Commit to continually moving more and more toward a humble compassion for all who are lost, regardless of their nationality.

9. Ask God to help you take steps toward your life being a continual offering for His purposes.

{God, I'm thankful for the example of Jonah. I confess I am much more like Him than I would care to admit. Yet, You faithfully loved Jonah, despite his failures. Thank You for Your steadfast love toward me. Make me more like Your Son as I walk forward in obedience to what You've shown me in Your Word. I praise Your glorious name.}

IF YOU HAVE MORE TIME . . .

Summation

Spend additional time in commentaries.

Add a title to this section in your outline in the appendix on page 174.

Pull out your journal and continue the conversation with God about what He is teaching you.

Share what you are learning with a trusted friend. Ask them to pray for you as you apply what you've learned.

List all the actions and experiences of Jonah, organize them chronologically, then sync them with the timeline you created for the actions of God on page 119.

WEEK 5: POINTS TO PONDER

[FOCUSING ON JONAH 4]

Be honest in prayer.

JONAH'S PRAYER IN verses 2 and 3 is nothing if not honest. Yes, Jonah's words are loathsome, but he has at least learned not to attempt hiding from God. Hiding from God resulted in the worst experience of his life. Now Jonah says what he feels even though his feelings reveal a deep-rooted sinfulness. God is big enough to handle your complaints and frustrations. Be authentic in prayer and pour your heart out to Him. He can take it.

Anger is pointless.

God disarms Jonah with one simple question, "Do you do well to be angry?" (Jonah 4:4). God asks Jonah if being angry produces the results he desires. Anger is a base response that even children are capable of. Most of us are so used to responding in anger that we have never thought about God's question. Have you ever stopped to think if your anger actually gets you anywhere? Usually our anger pushes away those who we seek to bring close. In other cases anger causes us to make more mistakes, which causes us to be angrier. God's question to Jonah is one we would all do well to ask when angry.

Hold things with an open hand.

The plant is a gift from God to Jonah; it protects him from the sun. As quickly as the plant appears it disappears, and Jonah is livid. It is easy for us to sit in judgment over Jonah, but how often do we get bent out of shape when a car breaks down, a loved one gets sick, or we receive an unexpected bill? Everything we have is from God, and nothing is ours to keep forever. This is why the New Testament refers to our handling of money and possessions as stewardship. A steward does not own an item; he merely manages it. By holding our possessions with a clinched fist we demonstrate our love for it is greater than our love for God. Enjoy God's gifts while they are entrusted to you, manage them well, and then be open to releasing them when God calls you to.

Humans are more important to God than any other living thing.

This may seem obvious to some of you, yet scandalous to others. Let me put the latter half of you at ease. We should not mistreat animals or the environment. We should steward all of God's creation well. However, the overwhelming testimony of the Bible is that humans carry the image of God in a way no plant or animal ever could. God values people more than He values other living things. Jonah is rebuked in chapter 4 because he confuses this priority. Jonah cares more for the plant than he does for the 120,000 souls in Nineveh. It is not wrong to love animals or nature, but Christ died for people, God gives His image to people, and the Holy Spirit dwells inside people. Value people even more than you value other aspects of God's creation.

WEEK 5: CHEAT SHEET

Day 2: Observation

2. Start by reading Jonah 4:1–4. Pay special attention to Jonah and the attitudes and emotions he conveyed about God's decision to show mercy to the nation of Nineveh.

ATTITUDES AND EMOTIONS OF JONAH IN 4:1-4

Displeased by God's relenting from showing His wrath to the Ninevites (v. 1)

Prayed/complained to God about His choice to be merciful (vv. 2–3)

States that the reason why he originally ran was because He knew God would show the Ninevites mercy (v. 2)

He'd rather die than live, because of what God has done (v. 3)

He was angry (v. 4)

3. Now focus on Jonah 4:5–9, looking at Jonah's attitudes and emotions toward God's appointment of the plant and the worm.

ATTITUDES AND EMOTIONS OF JONAH IN 4:5-9

Sat waiting to see what would become of the city—he's still hoping for God's destruction of Nineveh (v. 5)

Exceedingly glad for the plant God provided (v. 6)

Asked again to die, because God took away the shade of the plant and sent the scorching east wind (v. 8)

Angry over the loss of the plant—angry enough to die (v. 9)

Day 3: Clarification

4. Fill in the Hebrew chart for the original word you found for *pity*.

HEBREW WORD:	VERSE AND VERSION:
hws/hasta, chuwc/khoos	Jonah 4:10, 11 ESV

Part of Speech:
(verb, noun, etc.)

verb

Translation Notes:
(How else is it translated? How often is this word used?)

hws/hasta *is used ten times,* chuwc/khoos *is used 11 times. Though they look very different, these two are the same root word in Hebrew.*

Strong's Concordance Number:

H2347

Definition:

to be troubled; to look compassionately on; to spare

Notes:

"take pity, show mercy, have compassion, with a focus on sparing or delivering one from a great punishment" [James Swanson, Dictionary of Biblical Languages with Semantic Domains: Hebrew (Old Testament). Oak Harbor: Logos Research Systems, Inc., 1997]

WEEK 6

FOCUSING ON
THE CHARACTER OF GOD

Oh, that we might know the LORD! Let us press on to know him. He will respond to us as surely as the arrival of dawn or the coming of rains in early spring.

—Hosea 6:3 NLT

CHRIS HAS SAID for years that the most memorable weddings are the ones where something funny or awful happens. I've (Katie) come to believe he is right. As I look back on all the weddings I've attended, there is one that stands out the most. As the pastor began his sermon leading into the vows, he talked about the honorable characteristics of the bride and groom, and this is where things went all wrong. He used the best man's name instead of the groom's!

The pastor meant nothing by it. It was a simple slip of the tongue, but it caused a ripple of giggles throughout the church from those who caught the mess-up. Names are important. If Chris called me by the wrong name, I'm not going to jump for joy. When someone who I've known for years calls me Kathy instead of Katie, it bothers me. I'm assuming it would bother you too.

We've all heard bad sermons and wrong teachings. Unfortunately, we don't always recognize they are false because we don't know the Word well enough to recognize the bad theology. We call God by the wrong name without realizing it.

With a view toward knowing God better and better each day, we will spend our last week together looking at the character of God displayed in the Book of Jonah. By now, we hope you feel comfortable enough with the study method to use it on any passage you come across. This week, instead of staying in the same passage, we will look at a smaller group of verses each day and go through each part of our FOCUS method in one day.

FOUNDATION

Enjoy Every Word
> *Read and rewrite the passage*

OBSERVATION

Look at the Details
> *Take notes on what you see*

CLARIFICATION

Uncover the original meaning
> *Decide - Discover - Define*

UTILIZATION

Discover the connections
> *Cross-reference*

SUMMATION

Respond to God's Word
> *Identify - Modify - Glorify*

FOCUSING ON THE CHARACTER OF GOD

[EXPERIENCING GOD'S PRESENCE]

For you make him most blessed forever; you make him glad with the joy of your presence.

—Psalm 21:6

JONAH MISTAKENLY THOUGHT he could escape God's presence. He also missed that though he was scared to move forward in obedience, the most secure place to be is in the middle of God's plan. If He calls us to a task, He will provide for it. Additionally, the task is often not just about what it looks like at first glance. Oftentimes, God has a greater purpose in store—one we would never dream of on our own. Whether that greater purpose is revealed right away or it is one we will understand on the other side of eternity, obedience will always draw our hearts nearer to God's presence. And God's presence is ultimately the only thing that will satisfy, delight, and embolden our hearts.

Read the following verses and apply the FOCUS method to each.

1 Chronicles 16:11

Psalm 16:11

Acts 3:19–20

IF YOU
HAVE MORE
TIME . . .

FOCUS on

Psalm 24:3–7 and/or 27:8

FOCUSING ON THE CHARACTER OF GOD

[GOD'S SOVEREIGN PROVISION]

And my God will supply every need of yours according to his riches in glory in Christ Jesus.

—Philippians 4:19

GOD BROUGHT THE storm and its calm, the fish and dry land, as well as the plant, worm, and scorching wind into Jonah's life. He appointed each with purpose for Jonah's growth and sanctification (a big fancy word for becoming more like Jesus).

Our God is the creator, ruler, and sustainer of all we see and experience. From the ground we walk on to the air we breathe, it is all of God. God holds great power over nature—even when it seems out of control—and He uses His creation to fulfill His purposes in our lives. We see this truth clearly in the story of Jonah, as well as many other passages in Scripture.

After you begin your time in prayer, read Job 37:10–12 and Psalm 148:7–8 and apply the FOCUS method to these verses.

Job 37:10–12

Psalm 148:7–8

FOCUS on

Proverbs 3:19–20 and/or Jeremiah 10:12–13

FOCUSING ON THE CHARACTER OF GOD

[GOD'S PATIENCE WITH THE PERISHING]

> Therefore the LORD waits to be gracious to you, and therefore he exalts himself to show mercy to you. For the LORD is a God of justice; blessed are all those who wait for him.
>
> —Isaiah 30:18

NO ONE REJOICES when a guilty man doesn't receive the punishment he deserves. A good judge convicts the guilty, and you and I are as guilty as can be. We've offended a holy, righteous God—the eternal, righteous Judge. Christ paid the penalty for our sin so we could have a chance at a restored relationship with God. Through repentance and faith in Christ's work on the Cross, we can stand before our holy Judge and be declared innocent.

It is a glorious truth that is difficult to comprehend, but we ought to understand enough to realize the weight of God's holiness and the absolute wickedness of our sin. God has been patient with us in order to give a chance of redemption through Christ. God was patient with the Ninevites and their great transgressions. God continues to show Himself patient to those in our world today who are perishing without Christ.

Open your time in the Bible with prayer. FOCUS on 2 Peter 3:9 and Matthew 9:35–38.

2 Peter 3:9

Matthew 9:35–38

FOCUS on

Isaiah 30:18 and/or Numbers 14:18–19

FOCUSING ON THE CHARACTER OF GOD

[GOD'S PATIENCE WITH JONAH]

As a father shows compassion to his children, so the LORD shows compassion to those who fear him.

—Psalm 103:13

AT FIRST GLANCE, Jonah seems like an average guy who just didn't feel like preaching. We hope you've seen by now that this is far from the truth. Jonah was dealing with deep, wicked, heart-level issues. God was certainly patient with the people of Nineveh. He sent a warning and gave them a chance to repent. But He was also extremely patient with Jonah. Jonah may have been a well-behaved Hebrew who "feared" Yahweh, but his heart was far from emulating the compassion of God for the people of Nineveh. Jonah was able to manage his external obedience, but his heart was a wicked mess.

God didn't have to use Jonah to preach to the Ninevites. The moment Jonah ran, God could have left him to his new life in Tarshish. But God didn't. He pursued Jonah. God had a plan to show mercy and grace to the people of Nineveh, but He also had a plan to show mercy and grace to Jonah.

God has a plan for each of us as well. That is why He continues to show mercy and grace to us, even when our hearts are as wickedly messy as Jonah's.

Open your time with God in prayer, then spend some time reading through Romans 8:31–35 and FOCUS on these verses.

Romans 8:31–35

SUMMATION

[MOVING FORWARD IN OBEDIENCE]

WELL, YOU MADE it! Our study of Jonah is complete. We pray you have experienced a fresh look at the presence, provision, and patience of God through your time in His Word.

1. Let's look back and celebrate all we've learned and solidify our application in response. Take some time to glance through each week's summation day. Pay special attention to the "Modify" sections. Write out the application points you recorded for each week. Look for any themes in God's calling toward obedience.

WEEK 6 | DAY 5

It can be overwhelming when we dwell on of all the "work" that needs to be done in our hearts. We each fail every day. Oftentimes, in the same sin again and again. Thankfully, God has given us His Word with the truths we need to cling to.

2. Read 2 Peter 1:3 and observe what is true about God.

3. Look at 2 Peter 1:3 again. What does this verse say is true about you and me?

4. Now read Galatians 3:3, and look for the attitudes and actions Paul calls "foolish."

5. Lastly, read 1 John 5:14–15, and note the promise we are given.

We have everything we need for life and godliness. Everything. God does not call us to something on our own. We have His empowering, indwelling Spirit within us who gives us the desire to obey and the power to do what He calls us to (Philippians 2:13). And when we feel like we just can't do it, even when we read these truths? We pray. And we pray with confidence because God's will for us is to live an obedient life. We are charged with this over and over again—abide in Christ (John 15), walk by the Spirit (Galatians 5), and worship God through holy and pleasing lives (Romans 12:1). We can pray confidently to that end. He will answer that prayer!

6. To close your study, spend some time in prayer, asking God to clearly show you the step of obedience you need to take today. Ask Him to enable you to obey. Thank Him ahead of time for His patience, provision, and presence as you walk this journey of obedience.

Immersed in His grace, walk in confidence that your prayer to be more like Jesus will be answered.

CLOSING THOUGHTS

> The men of Nineveh will rise up at the judgment with this generation and condemn it, for they repented at the preaching of Jonah, and behold, something greater than Jonah is here.
>
> —Matthew 12:41

Though Jonah may not be on our list of heroes, this book and his story do point us to Christ. Where Jonah was faithless and cowardly, Jesus was willing and brave.

So yes, Jonah was a colossal failure. Yet God rescued him, corrected him, and used him—even in the midst of his great sin. We're all a bunch of failures—a disobedient group of prideful, compassionless, helpless sinners. But God has rescued us by His mercy. He corrects us out of love and uses us through His grace.

There is hope for us all.

We pray you will leave this Book of Jonah changed, with a greater perspective of who God is and who you are without Him. We also trust you feel a bit more confident in opening God's Word on your own. We're so grateful you've taken this journey with us. It is an honor to lead you closer to our Savior.

For His glory,

Chris and Katie Orr

{God, make our hearts softer, more willing to follow You regardless of the fears we may have to face.

Keep us clinging to You as our only hope, and may we live a life of awe-filled worship. A life where our actions line up with our declarations that Jesus is our King.

Continue to grant us repentance—an abiding sorrow over our sin and the ability to turn away from it.

May we be full of compassion for the lost and not be blinded by our pride or distracted by our comforts.

We are thankful for Your presence in our lives, Your patience with our journey, and Your provision for our every need.

Amen.}

BONUS STUDY WEEK

INTRODUCTION TO JONAH

Thus no other object on earth is as valuable as the Bible, for nothing else can provide anything as essential or eternal.
—DONALD WHITNEY, *TEN QUESTIONS TO DIAGNOSE YOUR SPIRITUAL HEALTH*

My son, if you receive my words and treasure up my commandments with you, making your ear attentive to wisdom and inclining your heart to understanding; yes, if you call out for insight and raise your voice for understanding, if you seek it like silver and search for it as for hidden treasures, then you will understand the fear of the LORD and find the knowledge of God.

—Proverbs 2:1–5

IN THE 1800s the American West experienced a gold rush. Thousands flocked across the continent in search of fortune and a better life. While many did indeed strike it rich, many others struck out altogether. Some even died on the journey to the fields of gold. In Canada, there was a similar rush for riches in the Yukon. This remote wilderness provided treasure seekers miles of untouched ground to seek their fortune.

In the early days of these expeditions, gold was easily found in streams and rivers. All a prospector needed was a pan and patience to pull from the water. When the waterways had been thoroughly picked over, new methods were required to get to the gold; prospecting gave way to mining. Now the prospectors would have to dig in order to get to the precious gold-bearing pay dirt. Mining is more difficult, more time consuming, and more expensive than the simple panning for gold on a riverbank. Many prospectors walked right over gold-laden dirt, looking for an easier way to get rich.

If you grew up going to church, chances are you are familiar with the story of Jonah. Familiarity can be one of our greatest enemies in the study of Scripture. If we believe we know what a passage says, we are much less likely to mine the depths of the riches contained in that text. Just like the gold rushers of old, if we believe all of the good stuff in Jonah has already been found we will be hesitant to dig in for ourselves. Yet, there are truths in the Book of Jonah you probably never learned in Sunday school.

One of the ways we will dig in for ourselves is by learning the context. In English class you learned about the five W questions: who, what, when, why, where (and how). All of these questions are designed to uncover the context before we begin looking at each chapter, verse-by-verse. Put down your pan and pick up a shovel. It is time to start digging.

DAY 1
A FIRST READ

I will meditate on your precepts and fix my eyes on your ways.

—Psalm 119:15

EACH FALL A local farming family creates an impressive corn maze. There is a super-simple kiddie maze, a longer, medium maze, and the complicated hour-long maze. Several years ago, I (Katie) attempted to take my younger kids and a few of their friends through the middle maze. Though it was only supposed to take ten to fifteen minutes, I got so turned around that after twenty minutes I found myself leading a bunch of crying kids around for an additional fifteen minutes. Eventually, I chose to cheat and sneak through the small spaces in the cornstalk walls back toward the sounds of civilization.

In the years since, I've decided to use the aerial-view map provided on their website, giving me a much better chance at getting through the maze without getting lost. Being able to see the patterns and knowing the general direction of the finish line grants me confidence in leading my kiddos through all the turns.

So it is with Bible study. Before we begin to study in depth, it is incredibly helpful for us to first get a good bird's-eye view of where we're headed.

Today we're going to read all of Jonah. That's it. Just sit back and enjoy. Don't try to overanalyze or dissect. Just read these four short chapters together, from start to finish.

We like to think of most Bible study to be in one of two categories: the bird's-eye view or the bug's life. We need both the big picture and the intricate details for a well-rounded study of Scripture. Remember, this week we're simply laying the foundation for the rest of our study. We'll dive in deep soon, we promise.

{Lord, I am thankful for Your Word and all it provides for my daily living. I am looking forward to diving into this little Book of Jonah. Continually open my eyes to the truths about You in these words. I long to know You better and follow You nearer.}

DAY 2
LOOKING AT THE WHEN

Make me understand the way of your precepts, and I will meditate on your wondrous works.

—Psalm 119:27

I (KATIE) HAVE come to love studying history, which is certainly not the case when I was in high school. I struggled to cram in dates and names, only to have them quickly leave my mind once the test was taken. Additionally, I was taught history in chopped-up segments, with no understanding of how each story and character fit in with the rest of the world. For all I knew, Joan of Arc, King Tut, and Abraham Lincoln lived at the same time.

Biblical history is often taught the same way in churches—as separate, singular stories. I was well into adulthood when I realized John the Baptist and the writer of the Book of John were two different people. It took me a long time to piece together that Abraham and Sarah were Joseph's great-grandparents. I had learned all about the journeys of Abraham and Isaac, knew the stories of Jacob and Esau, as well as the twelve sons of (Jacob) Israel. It wasn't until I began to read and study Scripture as a whole—instead of a bunch of separate parts—that I could see how these stories all wove together to reveal God's incredible story of redemption.

As we string together the stories of Scripture, we can learn more about each one through the association of the others.

1. Before we take a look at the contemporaries of Jonah and what was going on during his time, take a moment to ask for God's leading over your study time.

2. Do a quick read of 2 Kings 14:23–25, and write down what you learn about the following characters:

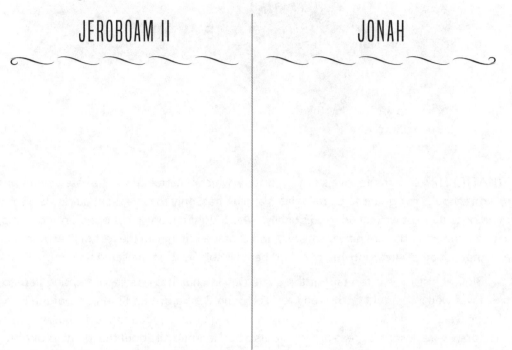

JEROBOAM II   JONAH

3. Take a quick peek at the Old Testament in a Nutshell chart in the appendix on page 175. Now, head back to 2 Kings 14:23–25, and look for clues that tell us at what time in history Jeroboam and Jonah lived. Write it below when you find it.

4. According to the timeline, where does the story of Jonah takes place?

You and I are blips. Teeny, tiny dots on the timeline of history. James calls us a mist that appears for a time, then disappears (James 4:13–15). Yet the tapestry of God's plan now and throughout history utilizes each small thread of a life and weaves into a beautiful display of His glory.

Pray to our tapestry-weaving God today, asking to see a glimpse of His plan for your life. Ask for the grace to remember your smallness and your great need for God's strength, guidance, and grace for today.

{God, You are faithful. As I look back on my own life, as well as the lives of generations, I can see Your constant, guiding, capable hand. I am so grateful for Your presence in my life.}

IF YOU HAVE MORE TIME . . .

Look up the following people and places in a Bible dictionary, or Google them and note anything interesting you learn about each.

Kings of Israel

Jeroboam II

Nineveh

Assyrian Empire

Joppa

Tarshish

DAY 3
LOOKING AT THE WHERE

Give me understanding, that I may keep your law and observe it with my whole heart.

—Psalm 119:34

I (KATIE) LOVE to travel. If the Lord allows, I would love to tour through Europe and trek through Africa. [I (Chris) would enjoy that too but can't imagine how we will ever pay for it!] We've been to Mexico, Haiti, and China on mission trips. The time spent at each was not near long enough. Meeting new people, experiencing new cultures, and tasting new foods brings a new perspective of God's heart for every tribe, tongue, and nation. It's one thing to hear about the Great Wall of China or see it in textbook pictures or on a Google search. It's another thing altogether to climb its steep, uneven steps and sit in the windowsill of the parapets and overlook the green Asian mountainside. After seeing the giant barrier with my own eyes, I can better comprehend the cost of labor and dynastic riches expended to complete such a feat.

Much of history can be understood better through geography. The significance of culture, battles, kingdoms, and crops is influenced by its location on the global landscape. Much of the Bible can also be better understood through geography, and there is much missed in our studies without a good knowledge of the physical settings of the stories.

1. Take a moment to ask God for focus as you peek at the "where" of the book of Jonah.

2. Look up the following cross references to learn more about Nineveh. Note your observations. Don't get bogged down with trying to find the "right answers." Just read and note anything you learn about Nineveh. Remember to consult the cheat sheet at the end of this week's study if you need some help.

2 Kings 19:36

Nahum 1:1

3. Using a map in your Bible, a Bible dictionary with maps, or a quick Google search of "Nineveh during the time of Jonah" for reference, find the Assyrian Empire in the map below, then locate Nineveh within that Empire. Label the map with what you've found. (Remember the cheat sheet if you get stuck!)

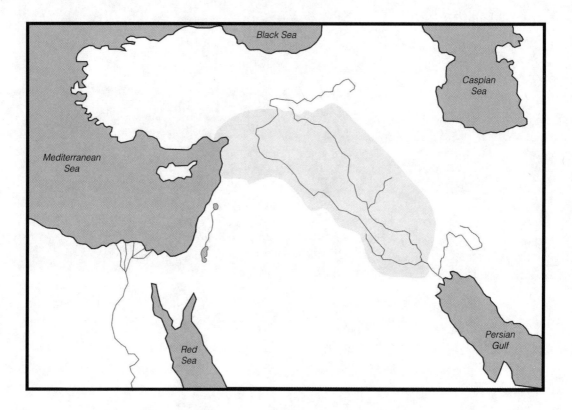

4. Read Jonah 1:3, and look for the other places in Jonah's story. Using your Bible, dictionary, or Google (search for "Tarshish during the time of Jonah"), find each location on the map and mark them on the map above. (While the exact location of Tarshish isn't known, indicate on the map with an arrow the general direction Tarshish can be found.)

The geography of our story reveals much about the flight of Jonah. Instead of ground travel to Nineveh, Jonah opted for a seaward sail in the opposite direction. He didn't simply ignore God's call, He attempted to flee far, far away. He failed to see that God's presence cannot be escaped, and His plans cannot be thwarted. No matter how far we run.

{God, I confess my view of Your presence is often way too small, and my desire to do Your will is often lacking. Thank You for placing me exactly where You have planted me. I want to be used for Your purposes. Be glorified through me.}

IF YOU HAVE MORE TIME . . .

Look up these additional cross references about Nineveh:

Zephaniah 2:13

Matthew 12:41

Luke 11:30

Read Genesis 10:8–12 to discover the founder of Nineveh. Note all you can learn about him.
Read Genesis 10:1 and 6. Read about and draw a simple family tree.

DAY 4
LOOKING AT THE OUTLINE

Open my eyes, that I may behold wondrous things out of your law.

—Psalm 119:18

RECENTLY I (KATIE) finally dove into a much-needed reorganization of our boys' bedroom. Eventually, it became an all-hands-on-deck situation as bags were filled with clothes and toys we no longer used, seasonal clothes were placed in closet bins, and mismatched socks found their mates. Through the sorting, purging, and establishing of new homes for each item in the room, we were able to consolidate down to one dresser instead of two. This opened up more room for the boys to enjoy their shared space.

As we continue to prepare to study each verse in the book of Jonah, we are going to begin organizing. We've taken an aerial view so far, and we have one more layer to enjoy today before we begin our descent to ground level.

1. Open your time in prayer, asking God for clarity and focus as you dive into the structure of Jonah.

2. Read through Jonah a chapter at a time and attempt to organize the book. As a shift in the narrative occurs, take note and try to section the book out in chunks. Give each chunk a title or summary statement for what has occurred. If this task is overwhelming for you, do an online search for an outline of the Book of Jonah (or peek at ours in the cheat sheet), then copy down one of the outlines you find. There are multiple ways to organize the story. Don't get hung up with trying to figure out the "right answer." You might think of it like scenes of a movie or play.

This week may seem slow for some of you. You might be ready to dive into the details. I'm the same way. Yet I've learned that taking time to understand the context and overall structure of a book provides a deeper study in the long run. Seeing a city overhead from a plane or having a snapshot of its grid grants me better navigation of the highways and streets. So does seeing the structure of a book help us better handle the Word.

{God, I long to rightly handle Your Word. Keep me from errant conclusions and bad theology. I'm grateful Your Word does not return to me void but brings abundant fruit for Your glory.}

DAY 5
JONAH IN THE NEW TESTAMENT

I cling to your testimonies, O Lord; let me not be put to shame!

—Psalm 119:31

SOME STORIES AND truths in Scripture are hard to fathom, and it can cause this analytical, science-loving soul (Katie) to wrestle with the validity of biblical narrative when lined up to the laws of nature. The flood, plagues of Egypt, and the parting of the Red Sea and then the Jordan river defy what modern science states as possible. People being raised from the dead, the blind being made to see, and the sick being completely healed are all mind-blowing. Then we have Jonah, who was swallowed by some sort of huge sea creature, dwelled within that giant for three days, and lived to tell the tale.

The Bible is filled with the accounts of the impossible. There are critics who say the biblical account of Jonah is simply an allegory—a story created by the writer to explain spiritual truths—but not a true, historical event. If I'm honest, I can see the attractiveness of this theory. Mainly because the likelihood of a man living inside of a fish for three days or a plant growing to maturity and dying in a 24-hour period seems completely absurd.

But our God is a God of power and impossibilities. He is not bound to the laws of nature. He created all we've come to know through science, and as the Creator of all, He can stop processes, suspend time, and create or destroy as He wills. He is a magnificent and mighty God, and though I have not seen with my own eyes a man being spit up from the belly of a fish, I have seen God do mighty works in my life. I have known His transforming work in countless of lives and have experienced fruit come forth from my life that has no other explanation than a movement of His Spirit.

Seeing His transformational work in my life and the lives of others gives me confidence in His ability to do much greater things.

1. Spend some time thinking back on your own conversion and journey with God. Thank Him for His powerful work within you. Confess any doubts you have about the validity of His Word, and ask Him to grant you a deep and abiding confidence in His ability to do wonders this world has never seen.

Though we must learn to walk by faith and not by sight (2 Corinthians 5:7), we do have several places in the New Testament that allow us to see the validity of the story of Jonah as a true, historic event. Let's take a look at these verses.

2. Read Matthew 12:38–42, and record what Jesus says about Jonah.

3. This account of Jesus' response to the scribes' request for a sign is also recorded in Luke 11:29. Read it, and add to your list any additional details you see.

Like most of their interactions with the Messiah, the question the scribes had for Jesus was rooted in distrust and a desire to breed dissension. They doubted Jesus was the Messiah, and their request for a sign had everything to do with them attempting to discredit Jesus.

4. Read 2 Timothy 3:14–17 and Romans 15:4, and list what is true of God's Word.

Jonah was written with great purpose. This story holds much for us to see, and I'm excited to see how God will use the life of Jonah—his mistakes and virtues—to speak truth to our hearts over the next five weeks.

{Lord, I praise You for Your faithful work in my life. Thank You for the provision of Your written Word. I confess my feeble mind sometimes allows doubt to creep in about the validity of Your Word. Grant me a firm conviction in every word, every story, and every truth You've given me through Scripture. By Your grace, I will stand on the promises to come and Your faithfulness past.}

BONUS STUDY: CHEAT SHEETS

Day 2: Looking at the When

2. Do a quick read of 2 Kings 14:23–25, and write down what you learn about the following characters:

JEROBOAM II	JONAH
Reigned in the 15th year of Amaziah (king of Judah)	Spoke the word of the Lord
Son of Joash	Servant of God
King of Israel	Son of Amittai
Reigned in Samaria	Prophet
Reigned 41 years	From Gath-hepher
Did evil in the sight of the Lord	
Restored some borders of Israel	

3. Take a quick peek at the Old Testament in a Nutshell chart in the appendix on page 175. Now, head back to 2 Kings 14:23–25, and look for clues that tell us at what time in history Jeroboam and Jonah lived. Write it below when you find it.

> *15th year of Amaziah's reign (v. 23)*
>
> *There is reference to kings of both Judah and Israel (v. 23)*
>
> *The kingdom's borders were restored by Jeroboam (v. 25)*
>
> *Since there is a reference to King Amaziah of Judah, we know Jeroboam led the nation of Israel after the split of Israel into two kingdoms.*

4. According to the timeline, where does the story of Jonah takes place?

> *After the split of the nation of Israel and before Assyria invaded.*

Day 3: Looking at the Where

2. Look up the following cross references to learn more about Nineveh. Note your observations.

2 Kings 19:36

> *home of Sennacherib, king of Assyria*

Nahum 1:1

> *The Book of Nahum is a record of the prophet Nahum's "oracle" also against Nineveh, like Jonah.*

3. Find the Assyrian Empire in the map below, then locate Nineveh within that Empire.

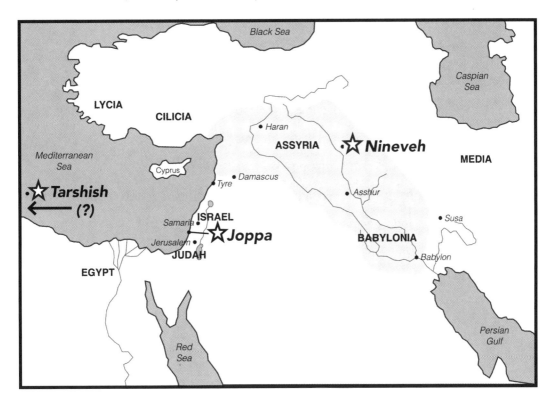

4. Read Jonah 1:3, and look for the other places in Jonah's story. Find each location on the map. (See Joppa and Tarshish in map above.)

Day 4: Looking at the Outline

2. Read through Jonah a chapter at a time and attempt to organize the book. As a shift in the narrative occurs, take note and try to section the book out in chunks. Give each chunk a title or summary statement for what has occurred.

Chris's outline of Jonah:

> 1:1-6 Jonah's run from assignment of God
>
> 1:7-17 Jonah's consequence for faithlessness
>
> 2 Jonah's prayer for deliverance
>
> 3 Jonah's ministry in Nineveh
>
> 4 Jonah's calloused heart toward people and the purposes of God

Katie's outline of Jonah:

> 1:1-3 God commissions Jonah to Nineveh; Jonah runs
>
> 1:4 God intervenes in Jonah's flight
>
> 1:5-16 Pagan sailors come to fear God; Jonah relents from his running
>
> 1:17 God provides a fish to save Jonah
>
> 2:1-9 Jonah prays to God from belly of fish
>
> 2:10 God delivers—commands the fish to spit Jonah onto dry land
>
> 3:1-4 God recommissions; Jonah obeys
>
> 3:5-9 Nineveh repents
>
> 3:10 God relents
>
> 4:1-5 Jonah angers over God's compassion
>
> 4:6-11 God appoints a lesson of rebuke

Day 5: Looking at Jonah in the New Testament

2. Read Matthew 12:38–42, and record what Jesus says about Jonah.

- *A prophet*
- *A given sign*
- *Spent three days and three nights in the belly of a great fish*
- *Likened to the Son of Man's (Jesus') death, burial, and Resurrection on the third day*
- *Preached to Nineveh, who repented*
- *A foreshadowing of greater things to come*

3. This account of Jesus' response to the scribes' request for a sign is also recorded in Luke 11:29. Read it, and add to your list any additional details you see.

- *Jonah is given to the generation as a sign.*
- *Jonah became a sign to the people of Nineveh, just as Christ would be a sign to that generation.*
- *Something greater than Jonah is here.*

4. Read 2 Timothy 3:14–17 and Romans 15:4, and list what is true of God's Word.

2 Timothy 3:14–17

- *Able to make you wise for salvation, through faith in Jesus Christ*
- *God-breathed*
- *Profitable for*
    Teaching
    Reproof
    Correction
    Training in righteousness

- Brings

   Completeness

   Equipping for every good work

Romans 15:4

- For our instruction
- Encouragement
- Brings hope

APPENDIX

OUTLINE OF JONAH

As you study, fill in the chart below with a title that summarizes each portion of Scripture.

JONAH 1:1-6

JONAH 1:7-16

JONAH 1:17
AND 2:1-10

JONAH 3

JONAH 4

OLD TESTAMENT IN A NUTSHELL

c. 5000 BC

Creation—God creates all things culminating in making man in His own image.

The Fall of Mankind—Mankind sins and rebels against God.

Noah and the Flood—The corruption of mankind increases, is judged by a global flood.

Tower of Babel—Mankind attempts to build their way to God. God separates people into distinct languages.

c. 1800 BC

Call of Abraham—God chooses a family through which He will bless the world, tells them to go to Canaan.

Era of the Patriarchs—Abraham, his son Isaac, and Isaac's son Jacob/Israel.

Twelve Tribes Established—Jacob's named changed to Israel. Jacob's sons become the fathers of all twelve of Israel's tribes.

Israel to Egypt—Jacob's son Joseph is sold into slavery, ends up second in command in Egypt and rescues his family from a major famine. All of the Hebrews move to Egypt.

Israelite Bondage—The Israelites become captive to Egypt, are subjected to forced labor.

c. 1440 BC
or
c. 1260 BC

The Exodus—God calls Moses to lead the Israelites out of bondage in Egypt.

The Desert Wanderings—The Israelites fail to trust God to deliver them into the Promised Land and are forced to wander in the wilderness for forty years.

The Law Given—God gives Moses the Law by which Israel is to live, including the Ten Commandments, sacrificial system, and how to build the Tabernacle.

The Conquest of the Promised Land—After Moses's death, God calls Joshua to lead the people into Canaan by driving out the Canaanite inhabitants.

The Period of Judges—God raises up judges to rule, and deliver Israel from foreign enemies.

c. 1043 BC

The Monarchy Established—Israel demands a king. God calls Saul to be the first king of Israel.

c. 1000–931 BC

The Golden Age—After Saul's disobedience, God anoints David king. David and his son Solomon lead Israel into prosperity and peace from its enemies.

The Temple Built—Solomon builds a permanent structure for the presence of God to dwell.

c. 931 BC

The Kingdom Divided—After Solomon's death Israel divides into two kingdoms. The northern tribes form Israel, the southern tribes form Judah.

c. 722 BC

The Destruction of Israel—The northern kingdom of Israel fails to obey God, becomes increasingly wicked. God judges Israel by allowing Assyria to invade.

c. 586 BC

The Exile of Judah—After the Babylonians overthrow the Assyrians, they invade Jerusalem, destroying the Temple and taking Judah into captivity.

c. 516 BC

The Return of the Jews—Persians defeat Babylon, Jews allowed to return to Jerusalem to rebuild the Temple.

GLOSSARY OF BIBLE STUDY TERMS

▪ **Interlinear Bible:** a translation where each English word is linked to its original Greek/Hebrew word. There are many free interlinear Bibles online, as well as great apps you can download to your phone or tablet. Check out KatieOrr.me/Resources for current links.

▪ **Concordance:** a helpful list of words found in the original languages of the Bible (mainly Hebrew and Greek) and the verses where you can find them.

▪ **Cross-reference:** a notation in a Bible verse that indicates there are other passages that contain similar material.

▪ **Footnote:** a numerical notation that refers readers to the bottom of a page for additional information.

▪ **Commentary:** a reference book written by experts that explains the Bible. A good commentary will give you historical background and language information that may not be obvious from the passage.

▪ **Greek:** the language in which most of the New Testament was written.

▪ **Hebrew:** the language in which most of the Old Testament was written.

STRUCTURE AND BOOKS OF THE BIBLE
Old Testament

» **Books of the Law (also known as the Pentateuch)**

Genesis	Numbers
Exodus	Deuteronomy
Leviticus	

» **Books of History**

Joshua	2 Kings
Judges	1 Chronicles
Ruth	2 Chronicles
1 Samuel	Ezra
2 Samuel	Nehemiah
1 Kings	Esther

» **Wisdom Literature**

Job	Ecclesiastes
Psalms	Song of Songs
Proverbs	

» **Major Prophets**

Isaiah	Ezekiel
Jeremiah	Daniel
Lamentations	

» **Minor Prophets**

Hosea	Nahum
Joel	Habakkuk
Amos	Zephaniah
Obadiah	Haggai
Jonah	Zechariah
Micah	Malachi

New Testament

⇢ Narratives (First four together are known as "The Gospels")

Matthew	John
Mark	Acts
Luke	

⇢ Epistles (or Letters) by Paul

Romans	1 Thessalonians
1 Corinthians	2 Thessalonians
2 Corinthians	1 Timothy
Galatians	2 Timothy
Ephesians	Titus
Philippians	Philemon
Colossians	

⇢ General Epistles (Letters not by Paul)

Hebrews	1 John
James	2 John
1 Peter	3 John
2 Peter	Jude

⇢ Apocalyptic Writing

Revelation

MAJOR THEMES OF THE BIBLE

Though many view Scripture as a patchwork of historical accounts, morality tales, and wisdom for daily living, the Bible is really only one story—the mind-blowing story of God's plan to rescue fallen humanity. This storyline flows through every single book, chapter, verse, and word of Scripture. It's crucial that we know the movements, or themes, of the grand storyline so we don't miss the point of the passage we are studying.

For example, I grew up hearing the story of David's adulterous affair with the beautiful, but married, Bathsheba. I heard how he covered his misdeeds with a murderous plot to snuff out her husband. This story was usually punctuated with a moral that went something like this, "Don't take what isn't yours!" While it is indeed good practice to refrain from taking what isn't ours, there is a much bigger connection to the grand story that we will miss if we stop at a moral lesson. So what then is this grand story, and how can we recognize it?

The story falls into four main themes, or movements: creation, fall, redemption, and completion*.

Creation

The Bible begins by describing the creative work of God. His masterwork and crowning achievement was the creation of people. God put the first couple, Adam and Eve, in absolute paradise and gave them everything they needed to thrive. The best part of this place, the Garden of Eden, was that God walked among His people. They knew Him and were known by Him. The Bible even says they walked around naked because they had no concept of shame or guilt. (See Genesis 2:25.) Life was perfect, just like God had designed.

Fall

In the Garden, God provided everything for Adam and Eve. But He also gave them instructions for how to live and established boundaries for their protection. Eventually, the first family decided to cross a boundary and break the one rule God commanded them to keep. This decision was the most fateful error in history. At that precise moment, paradise was lost. The connection that people experienced with God vanished. Adam and Eve's act was not simply a mistake but outright rebellion against the sovereign Creator of the universe. It was, in no uncertain terms, a declaration of war against God. Every aspect of creation was fractured in that moment. Because of their choice, Adam and Eve

For a more detailed discussion on these themes, refer to Part 1 and 2 of The Explicit Gospel by Matt Chandler (pages 21–175) or Chapter 2 of Mark Dever's The Gospel and Personal Evangelism (pages 31–44).

introduced death and disease to the world, but more importantly, put a chasm between mankind and God that neither Adam nor Eve nor any person could ever hope to cross. Ever since the fall, all people are born with a tendency to sin. Like moths to a light, we are drawn to sin, and like Adam and Eve, our sin pushes us further away from any hope of experiencing God. You see God cannot be good if He doesn't punish sin, but if we all receive the punishment our sin deserves we would all be cast away from Him forever.

Redemption

Fortunately, God was not caught off guard when Adam and Eve rebelled. God knew they would and had a plan in place to fix what they had broken. This plan meant sending Jesus to earth. Even though Jesus was the rightful King of all creation, He came to earth in perfect humility. He walked the earth for more than thirty years experiencing everything you and I do. Jesus grew tired at the end of a long day. He got hungry when He didn't eat. He felt the pain of losing loved ones and the disappointment of betrayal from friends. He went through life like we do with one massive exception—He never sinned. Jesus never disobeyed God, not even once. Because He was without sin, He was the only one in history who could bridge the gap between God and us. However, redemption came at a steep price. Jesus was nailed to a wooden cross and left to die a criminal's death. While He hung on the Cross, God put the full weight of our sin upon Jesus. When the King of the universe died, He paid the penalty for our sin. God poured out His righteous anger toward our sin on the sinless One. After Jesus died, He was buried and many believed all hope was lost. However, Jesus did not stay dead—having defeated sin on the Cross, He was raised from death and is alive today!

Completion

The final theme in the grand storyline of the Bible is completion, the end of the story. Now that Jesus has paid the penalty for our sin, we have hope of reconciliation with God. This is such tremendous news because reconciliation means we are forgiven of sin and given eternal life. Reconciliation means God dwells with us again. Finally, we know Him and are known by Him. Completion for us means entering into reconciliation with God through the only means He provided. We can only experience reconciliation under God's rescue plan if we trust Jesus to pay for our sin and demonstrate this by repenting, or turning away, from our sin. But God's rescue plan does not end with us. One day, Jesus will come back and ultimately fix every part of fallen creation. King Jesus will come back to rule over God's people, and again establish a paradise that is free from the effects of sin.

Let's return to the David and Bathsheba story for a moment and try to find our place. David was the greatest, most godly king in the history of the Old Testament, but even he was affected by the fall and had a sinful nature. This story points out that what we really need is not a more disciplined eye but a total transformation. We need to be delivered from the effects of the fall. It also illustrates how we don't simply need a king who loves God, but we need a King who is God. Do you see how this story connects to the arc of the grand storyline? Just look at how much glorious truth we miss out on if we stop short at "don't take what isn't yours."

HOW TO DO A GREEK/HEBREW WORD STUDY

Learning more about the language used in the original version of Scripture can be a helpful tool toward a better understanding of the author's original meaning and intention in writing. The Old Testament was written in Hebrew and the New Testament in Greek. Though the thought of learning a new language is overwhelming to most of us, we live in an age with incredible tools at our fingertips through smartphone apps and online websites (many of which are free!) that make understanding the original meaning as simple as looking a word up in a dictionary.

Here are three easy steps to work toward a better understanding of the verses you study.

DECIDE which word you would like to study.

Do a quick read of your passage and note any potential keywords and/or repeated words. There is no right or wrong way to do this! Simply select a few words you would like to learn more about.

DISCOVER that word as it was originally written.

Using an interlinear Bible (see glossary), find the original Greek (if New Testament) or Hebrew (if Old Testament) word for each instance of the word in the passage you are studying. There may be more than one Greek or Hebrew word present that translated into one English word.

DEFINE that word.

Look up your Greek/Hebrew word (or words if you found more than one) in a Greek/Hebrew lexicon. Most of the free apps and websites available do this with a simple click of a button, opening up a wealth of information referenced from a lexicon they've chosen. I encourage you to check out the videos I've created to show you how to use many of the online Greek/Hebrew tools. You can find them at KatieOrr.me/Resources.

Though this step can seem overwhelming, once you find an app or site you love, it is as simple as looking up a word in the dictionary. Here is a chart you can use to record what you learn.

Greek/Hebrew Word Study Worksheet

GREEK/HEBREW WORD: VERSE AND VERSION:

Part of Speech: *(verb, noun, etc.)*	**Translation Notes:** *(How else is it translated? How often is this word used?)*
Strong's Concordance Number:	**Definition:**

Notes:

HOW TO DO A GREEK/HEBREW WORD STUDY—EXAMPLE

Let's walk through this process, looking at Hebrews 11:1 together. I've also included extra notes to help you better understand the behind-the-scenes work the apps and websites are doing for us.

DECIDE which word you would like to study.

Since Hebrews is in the New Testament, we'll be working with the Greek language. To start your Greek study, look for any potential keywords in Hebrews 11:1. As you find any repeated word or words that seem important to the passage, write them down.

faith, assurance, hoped, conviction, things, seen

Since faith is probably what the main point of this verse is about, let's study this word together.

DISCOVER that word as it was originally written.

Now that we know what we want to study, we can look up the English word *faith* in an interlinear Bible to find out what the original Greek word is. An interlinear Bible will show you English verses and line up each word next to the Greek words they were translated from. If you own or have seen a parallel Bible, with two or more English translation versions (ie, ESV, KJV, NIV) lined up next to each other, this is the same concept. Interlinear Bibles have the original language alongside an English translation.

Let's take the first phrase in Hebrews 11:1 to see how this works:

Now faith is the assurance of things hoped for. —Hebrews 11:1

In Greek, it looks like this: *ἔστιν δὲ πίστις ἐλπιζομένων.*

Most people (including me!) can't read this, so the transliteration of the Greek is often provided for us as well. This transliteration is simply the sound of each Greek letter turned into English letters to spell out how the Greek is read. It's a phonetic spelling of the Greek word. For example, the first Greek words we see, *ἔστιν* and *δὲ*, are transliterated into *estin* and *de*, which is how they are pronounced.

The interlinear Bible simply lines up the two versions (and typically the transliteration as well) so we can see which word goes with which, like this:

ἔστιν	δὲ	πίστις	ἐλπιζομένων
estin	de	pistis	elpizomenōn
is	now	faith	of things hoped for

Now you can use this layout to find the original word for *faith*. Do you see it?

Faith=pistis=πίστις

DEFINE that word.

Now that we know the original word for faith used in Hebrews 11:1 is *pistis*, we can look up that Greek word in a Greek lexicon (which is like a dictionary) and note what we learn about the original meaning of the word. I've provided a worksheet to record this info. *(For a free printable version of this worksheet, go to KatieOrr.me /Resources and look for the PRINTABLES section.)*

GREEK WORD:
pistis

VERSE AND VERSION:
Hebrews 11:1

Part of Speech:
(verb, noun, etc.)

noun

Translation Notes:
(How else is it translated? How often is this word used?)

used 243 times in the New Testament ESV. All but two times it is translated "faith." Other two translations: assurance (1) and belief (1)

Strong's Concordance Number:
G4102

Definition:
faith, confidence, fidelity, guarantee, loyalty

Notes:

pistis, which derives from peithomai ("be persuaded, have confidence, obey"), connotes persuasion, conviction, and commitment, and always implies confidence, which is expressed in human relationships as fidelity, trust, assurance, oath, proof, guarantee. Only this richness of meaning can account for the faith (pistei, kata pistin, dia pisteos) that inspired the conduct of the great Israelite ancestors of Hebrews 11.

THE GOOD NEWS

God Loves You

You are known and deeply loved by a great, glorious, and personal God. This God hand-formed you for a purpose (Ephesians 2:10), He has called you by name (Isaiah 43:1), and you are of great worth to Him (Luke 12:6–7).

We Have a Sin Problem

We are all sinners and are all therefore separated from God (Romans 3:23; 6:23). Even the "smallest" of sins is a great offense to God. He is a righteous judge who will not be in the presence of sin and cannot allow sin to go unpunished. Our natural tendency toward sin has left us in desperate need of rescue because God must deal with our sin.

Jesus Is the Only Solution

Since God's standard is perfection, and we have all fallen short of the mark, Jesus is the only answer to our sin problem (John 14:6). Jesus lived a life of perfect obedience to God. So when Jesus died on the Cross, He alone was able to pay the penalty of our sin.

After His death, Jesus rose from the dead, defeating death, and providing the one way we could be reconciled to God (2 Corinthians 5:17–21). Jesus Christ is the only one who can save us from our sins.

We Must Choose to Believe

Trusting Christ is our only part in the gospel. Specifically, the Bible requires us to have faith in what Christ has done on our behalf (Ephesians 2:8–9). This type of faith is not just belief in God. Many people grow up believing God exists but never enter into the Christian faith. Faith that saves comes from a desperate heart. A heart that longs for Jesus—the only solution for their sin problem—to be first and foremost in their life. We demonstrate that we have this type of saving faith by turning away, or repenting, from our sin.

FOCUSED15 STUDY METHOD

Apply this method to two to ten verses a day, over a week's time, for a deep encounter with God through His Word, in as little as fifteen minutes a day.

Foundation: Enjoy Every Word

Read and rewrite the passage—summarize, draw pictures, diagram sentences, or simply copy the passage. Do whatever helps you slow down and enjoy each word.

Observation: Look at the Details

Take notes on what you see—write down truths in this passage. Look for truths about the character of God, promises to cling to, or commands given.

Clarification: Uncover the Original Meaning

- **Decide which word you would like to study.**
  Look for any repeated words or keywords to look up, choose one, and learn more about it.

- **Discover that word as it was originally written.**
  Using an interlinear Bible, find the original Greek or Hebrew word for the English word you chose.

- **Define that word.**
  Learn the full meaning of the word using a Greek or Hebrew lexicon, which is very much like a dictionary.

Utilization: Discover the Connections

Cross-reference—Look up the references in each verse to view the threads and themes throughout the Bible.

Summation: Respond to God's Word

☞ **Identify—Find the main idea of the passage.**

☞ **Modify—Evaluate my beliefs in light of the main idea.**

☞ **Glorify—Align my life to reflect the truth of God's Word.**

Experience a Deeper Connection to God's Word

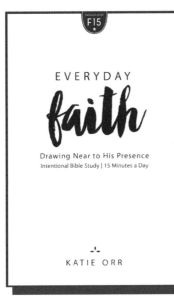

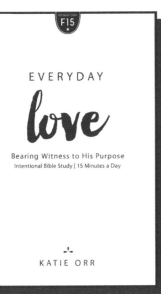
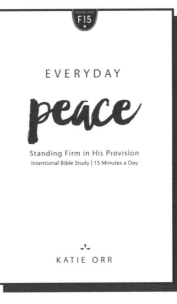
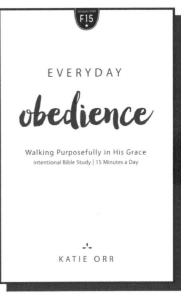

IF YOU ENJOYED THIS BOOK,
WILL YOU CONSIDER SHARING
THE MESSAGE WITH OTHERS?

Let us know your thoughts at **info@newhopepublishers.com**. You can also let the author know by visiting or sharing a photo of the cover on our social media pages or leaving a review at a retailer's site. All of it helps us get the message out!

 Twitter.com/NewHopeBooks

 Facebook.com/NewHopePublishers

 Instagram.com/NewHopePublishers

New Hope® Publishers is an imprint of **Iron Stream Media**, which derives its name from:

Proverbs 27:17, "As iron sharpens iron, so one person sharpens another."

This sharpening describes the process of discipleship, one to another. With this in mind, Iron Stream Media provides a variety of solutions for churches, missionaries, and nonprofits ranging from in-depth Bible study curriculum and Christian book publishing to custom publishing and consultative services. Through the popular Life Bible Study and Student Life Bible Study brands, ISM provides web-based full-year and short-term Bible study teaching plans as well as printed devotionals, Bibles, and discipleship curriculum.

For more information on ISM and New Hope Publishers, please visit

IRONSTREAMMEDIA.COM

NewHopePublishers.com